DISCOVERIES IN READING

CHALLENGES

BOOK 2

Sandra
McCandless
Simons

D1378442

HBJ

Harcourt Brace Jovanovich, Inc.

Holt, Rinehart and Winston, Inc.

Orlando · Austin · San Diego · Chicago · Dallas · Toronto

Acknowledgments

For permission to reprint copyrighted material, grateful acknowledgment is made to the following sources:

Bradbury Press, an affiliate of Macmillan, Inc.: "A Bad Road for Cats" from *Every Living Thing* by Cynthia Rylant. Text copyright © by Cynthia Rylant.

Harold Courlander: "The Sun Callers" from *People of the Short Blue Corn* by Harold Courlander. Text copyright © 1970 by Harold Courlander.

Greenwillow Books, a division of William Morrow and Company, Inc.: "The Kraken" from *The Headless Horseman Rides Tonight* by Jack Prelutsky. Text copyright © 1980 by Jack Prelutsky.

Bruce B. Henderson: "The Kids Who Saved a Dying Town" by Bruce B. Henderson from *Reader's Digest* Magazine, September 1987. Copyright © 1987 by Bruce B. Henderson.

Liveright Publishing Corporation: "who knows if the moon's" from *Tulips & Chimneys* by E. E. Cummings, edited by George James Firmage. Copyright 1923, 1925 and renewed 1951, 1953 by E. E. Cummings; copyright © 1973, 1976 by the Trustees for the E. E. Cummings Trust; copyright © 1973, 1976 by George James Firmage.

Macmillan Publishing Company: Adapted from "Questions and Answers About Your Body" (Retitled: "Goose Bumps and Funny Bones") in *Macmillan Illustrated Almanac for Kids* by Ann Elwood, Carol Orsag and Sidney Solomon. Copyright © 1981 by Ann Elwood, Carol Orsag and Sidney Solomon.

Macmillan Publishing Company and Faber and Faber Ltd.: "My Uncle Dan" from *Meet My Folks* by Ted Hughes. Copyright © 1961, 1973 by Ted Hughes.

McIntosh and Otis, Inc., on behalf of Donald J. Sobol: "The Case of the Last Moreno" and "The Case of the Blackmailer" from *Two-Minute Mysteries* by Donald J. Sobol. Copyright © 1967 by Donald J. Sobol. "The Case of the Unknown Brother" from *More Two-Minute Mysteries* by Donald J. Sobol. Copyright © 1967 by Donald J. Sobol. "The Case of the Dowager's Jewels" (Retitled: "The Case of the Stolen Jewels") from *Still More Two-Minute Mysteries* by Donald J. Sobol. Copyright © 1975 by Donald J. Sobol. All published by Scholastic Inc.

Random House, Inc.: Adapted from "The Midnight Visitor" in *Mystery and More Mystery* by Robert Arthur. Copyright 1939, renewed 1967 by Robert Arthur.

Marian Reiner, on behalf of Eve Merriam: "Thumbprint" from *A Sky Full of Poems* by Eve Merriam. Copyright 1964, 1970, 1973 by Eve Merriam. All rights reserved.

Raboo Rodgers: Adapted from "Out of the Silence" by Raboo Rodgers in *Boy's Life* Magazine, November 1980.

Beverly Ruuth: "A Dream to Run" By Beverly Ruuth from *Cricket* Magazine, August 1988. © 1988 by Beverly Ruuth.

Larry Sternig Literary Agency: "Zoo" by Edward D. Hoch. Copyright © 1958 by King-Size Publications, Inc.: copyright renewed © 1986 by Edward D. Hoch.

Dear Students,

If we could make a wish for you, we would wish for you always to be successful. We would wish that you would meet every challenge and succeed at everything you do. Because these are our wishes for you, we want to do whatever we can to make them come true.

One thing we can do is to provide you with the kind of stories and poems you will find in this book. They deal with characters—some real and some fictional—who must overcome challenges in their lives. Following their examples may help you meet your own personal challenges.

As you read, pay attention to the characters who suffer defeats and setbacks. Notice how each is able to bounce back from difficulty and to try again. That is one way to succeed in life—by turning losses into gains, setbacks into victories.

We have enjoyed working on these books for you. We wish you all the best as you continue your education.

Sincerely,
The Editors

CONTENTS

UNIT 1

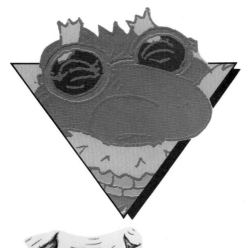

CONTENTS

UNIT 2

CONTENTS

UNIT 3

who knows
if the moon's
by E. E. Cummings (Poem)

A Dream to Run
by Beverly Ruuth
(Realistic Fiction)

CONTENTS

UNIT 4

Out of the Silence
by Raboo Rodgers
(Realistic Fiction)

The World Around Us
Students' Writing (Essays)

Unit 1

Working with a group of special performers turns out to be the right challenge for Diane Dupuy.

Burglars beware! You don't stand a chance against Dr. Haledjian, the master detective.

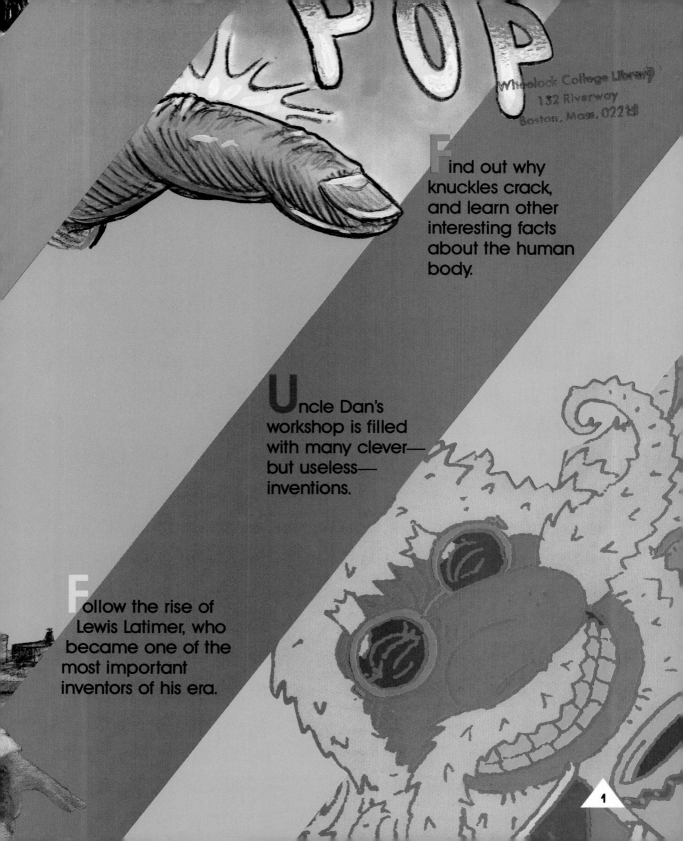

Find out why knuckles crack, and learn other interesting facts about the human body.

Uncle Dan's workshop is filled with many clever— but useless— inventions.

Follow the rise of Lewis Latimer, who became one of the most important inventors of his era.

THE RIGHT CHALLENGE

by Susan Sermoneta

Diane Dupuy needed the right challenge to give her life a meaningful direction. Discover how she found and shared her challenge with others.

t is September 1988. Diane Dupuy sits at her desk and reads *Variety,* the weekly newspaper for show-business professionals all over the world.

Diane turns to the back cover. There, against a black background, inch-high white letters of a headline seem to jump off the page:

HATS OFF TO DIANE DUPUY
ON HER 40TH BIRTHDAY!

Above the headline is a photograph of Diane's smiling face, nearly half a foot high. Her chin rests on her hands. Under the headline is a special message:

Happy Birthday, Diane. And congratulations on your continued success. . . . Through your love and dedication, the Famous People Players' *Colors in the Dark* has dazzled standing-room-only audiences at Sea World's Fantasy Theatre for a record-breaking 32 weeks.

Beneath the message are the signatures of dozens of friends. Well-wishers include the Famous People Players themselves. Ted's name is printed in letters of different sizes. Michelle's name, Lisa's name, and Renato's name are written in what look like the scrawls of little children.

Not every member of the troop has signed this special card. Not every one of the Famous People Players can write. Most of the Famous People Players are mentally handicapped. However, few of the enthusiastic fans in their audiences know it.

How can adults who are mentally handicapped be successful professionals? Diane would say it is because they have found the right challenge.

A DIFFICULT CHILDHOOD

Diane Dupuy was able to help the Famous People Players find the right challenge because she had found the right one for herself. It took Diane the first 25 years of her life to find this challenge.

When she was a little girl in Canada, Diane used her imagination like a magic wand. She changed one world into another.

Diane did poorly in her academic subjects. One day her teacher returned an arithmetic quiz. Out of 22 questions, Diane had missed 20.

Diane repeated whole years of school. She never got past the eighth grade.

Diane felt that most of her teachers disliked her. She was often teased by her classmates. At recess one day when she was only six, a group of classmates circled Diane. They chanted "Retard! Retard!" They made fun of her skinny body and big brown eyes.

Diane never defended herself. She spoke out only once. In seventh grade, a classmate had an epileptic seizure. The others laughed at the girl lying on the floor in a tangle of clothes. Diane, however, cried. Then she yelled at her classmates for their cruelty.

Diane's imagination usually consoled her. She says, "If I failed a test and got scolded or punished, or if the kids made fun of me after school, I just climbed on my imaginary horse, Silver, and galloped all the way home.

Only once did Diane use her imagination to win the applause of her classmates. For a birthday, Diane's mother had given her a puppet theater and the puppets Punch and Judy. In seventh grade, Diane put on a puppet show at school. Punch and Judy battled. Diane's classmates cheered. Diane says, "I didn't mind the bullies anymore because they were applauding me. I felt happy to be making others happy. But I didn't do any more puppet shows at school."

Not until she was 20 did Diane again let her imagination help her change her world. She rediscovered her puppets. She was searching through a hall closet for a pair of shoes. There were Punch and Judy and the theater. Diane remembered the warm feelings of loving those puppets. She remembered the applause.

With her mother's help, Diane became a part-time professional puppeteer. At first she put on shows in shopping malls. She got better and better. Diane invented skits using puppets of famous Canadians. She won a three-week run at the Canadian National Exhibition.

After one show, a member of the audience congratulated Diane. It was Bill Cosby. He told Diane about black-light puppet theater.

Diane went to the library. She read about black-light theater. Under black light, puppeteers in black clothing and hoods move invisibly around a darkened stage. Puppets painted with fluorescent colors come to life with incredible energy, magically dancing and gliding across the stage. Diane was fascinated. Later Diane's Famous People Players would use this very technique.

Now, however, Diane was busy giving her own puppet shows. One day the phone rang. Diane listened as a woman asked her to give a show at Surrey Place Centre, a home for children who were mentally handicapped.

Diane thought, *I don't want to do this. How did they get my name, anyway? These kids are going to be a bunch of crazies. They'll knock down the theater. They'll ruin the show. . . .* Her mind raced to her memories of kids shouting "Retard! Retard!" when she was six.

Diane said none of this on the telephone. Instead, she amazed herself by answering, "Yes, I'd be delighted to do it." That show, in February 1973, changed Diane's life.

THE WORLD OF PUPPETRY

A NEW DIRECTION

Fifty children in the audience at Surrey Place Centre laughed and cheered. These children were mentally handicapped. Yet they appreciated Diane's show with special sensitivity.

Enthusiastic fans were not new for Diane. What was new was the children's reaction to an emergency—an emergency Diane had seen before.

In the middle of the puppet show, one of the young people in the audience had an epileptic seizure. This time nobody laughed. Other youngsters rushed to the girl. They gently straightened her clothing. They made sure she hadn't hurt herself falling.

That did it. Diane volunteered time each week to work with the mentally handicapped.

For her volunteer training, Diane visited an institution for the mentally handicapped. There Diane saw bathrooms without doors. She watched the staff herd patients from one place to another. She looked into faces and saw that neither patients nor staff ever smiled. Diane felt horrified, sad, and angry.

Diane remembers, ''I wanted to somehow change the situation. I wanted to save these people. It was as if I were on my imaginary horse Silver again, riding like crazy to save a whole town. Only now the feeling was all caught up with my puppets and the pleasure they gave the children at Surrey Place, and the misery of the people in the institution.''

Diane made up her mind. She would start a black-light puppet theater company. The puppeteers would be young people who were mentally handicapped. They could have careers as professional performers. They could be self-sufficient adults.

Once she got started, there was no stopping Diane. Many people along the way tried to stop her. Only Diane actually believed that people who were mentally handicapped could be professional performers.

Against all odds, Diane succeeded in getting an Opportunities for Youth grant. It paid salaries and rent. Diane used her own salary for supplies.

Then Diane addressed a group of eleven teenagers who would join her company. They giggled and shouted uncontrollably throughout her talk. Most of them had severe speech impediments, so it took Diane an hour to collect their names. It took her another hour to make them understand where the first rehearsal would be.

It took Diane a full year to teach the company three 2-minute routines. Most puppets needed three people to manipulate them. Just teaching the performers to hold puppets and props right side up took months.

At last the Famous People Players gave their first public show: six minutes of performance and a twenty-minute speech by Diane.

The show started out fine; it ended in disaster. A few minutes into the performance, one of the puppeteers walked off the stage. Mass confusion erupted in the darkness. The performance limped on. At the end, a loud voice boomed from the audience, ''You guys were great!'' It was the missing puppeteer.

The performer-turned-fan had heard the applause for the first routine. He had thought to himself, *This show must really be good.* So he had joined the audience in order to see it.

A COMPANY OF PROFESSIONALS

Diane created new routines and, with her mother's help, added new puppets.

"Aruba Liberace,[1]" which used one of Liberace's recordings, had been the company hit from the start. A life-sized Liberace puppet danced and floated across the stage. Diane read that Liberace would perform soon in Toronto. With typical determination, she made up her mind to meet him and insist that he see their show.

Diane approached Liberace after his Toronto performance. She told him about the show and asked him to see it. He agreed!

The performance that Liberace attended went perfectly. Liberace laughed, wept, and enjoyed himself throughout. The performers took their final bows. Suddenly Liberace jumped up from his seat, ran to the stage, grabbed the microphone, and announced, "I've never seen anything so wonderful. I want these performers to come to Las Vegas and be part of my show!"

Liberace returned to his seat, and each of the performers approached him with a rose. Then Liberace realized that most of the Famous People Players were mentally handicapped. At that point, he returned to the microphone and added, "It's not because of who you are that people laugh or cry. It's because you're truly talented performers."

For eight years, the Famous People Players performed in Liberace's Las Vegas show. At first, stagehands wondered, *Who are these weird people?* Few could read or write. Few could tell a one-dollar bill from a five.

Yet everyone treated the Famous People Players as a company of professionals. The Famous People Players had gained the pride, the professionalism, and the self-sufficiency that Diane knew would come. They had been given the right challenge.

---

[1]Liberace [li•ber•ä•chē]: a famous pianist known for his flashy costumes and extravagant performances

A holiday run at Radio City Music Hall in New York City followed. Then came shows all over the world, including a performance tour in China. CBS made a movie, *Special People,* starring Brooke Adams as Diane Dupuy. Many of the Famous People Players played themselves. The performers were interviewed on television shows, including the "Phil Donahue Show."

Through these live interviews, the public learned about the special nature of the company. People began to treat the Famous People Players differently—like "retards." Stagehands spoke slowly, using limited vocabulary. Fans recognized the performers on the street and treated them like little children. The Famous People Players were upset.

Diane's solution was a new challenge. "Put on a major production. Don't tell the reviewers who we are."

So the hit Broadway show *A Little Like Magic* was born. *New York Times* drama critic Richard Shepard raved about the troop's magic. He added, "Not until the very end of *A Little Like Magic* do you see a full, normal human being." The company of professionals had done it again.

A NEW CHALLENGE

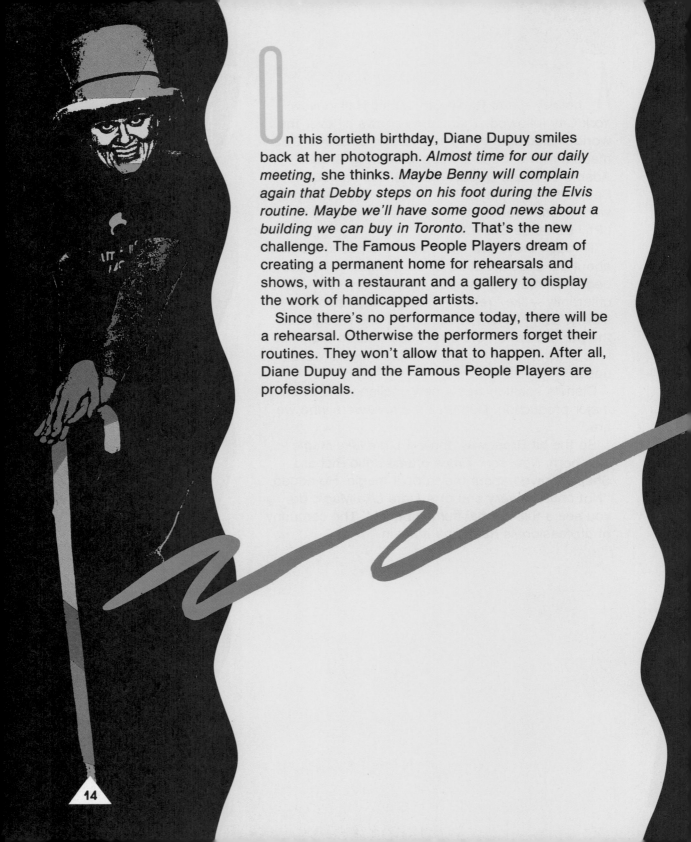

On this fortieth birthday, Diane Dupuy smiles back at her photograph. *Almost time for our daily meeting,* she thinks. *Maybe Benny will complain again that Debby steps on his foot during the Elvis routine. Maybe we'll have some good news about a building we can buy in Toronto.* That's the new challenge. The Famous People Players dream of creating a permanent home for rehearsals and shows, with a restaurant and a gallery to display the work of handicapped artists.

Since there's no performance today, there will be a rehearsal. Otherwise the performers forget their routines. They won't allow that to happen. After all, Diane Dupuy and the Famous People Players are professionals.

Talk about it!

1 What was the right challenge for Diane Dupuy? Why was it so appropriate for her?

2 How did Diane share her challenge with others?

3 How has your attitude toward mentally handicapped people been influenced by this true story? Explain your answer.

4 Diane Dupuy has accomplished a great deal for herself and for others despite many obstacles. How could her life serve as an inspiration to other people?

5 How do you know that Diane Dupuy is a person who does not give up easily?

Bibliography

A Handful of Stars by Barbara Girion. Scribner. Everything is going well for Julie Ann until epilepsy enters her life.

M.E. and Morton by Sylvia Cassidy. Crowell. Mary Ella and her mildly handicapped brother try to find imaginative freedom.

Hewitt's Just Different (film). Time-Life. Willie discovers something special about Hewitt, a sixteen-year-old mentally handicapped boy.

A LITTLE MYST

FROM

**TWO-MINUTE MYSTERIES,
MORE TWO-MINUTE MYSTERIES,
and STILL MORE TWO-MINUTE MYSTERIES**

BY **Donald J. Sobol**

ERVE

HAVE you ever wanted to know whether you'd make a good detective? Here's your chance to find out. Try your skill at solving each mystery along with Dr. Haledjian.[1]

---

[1]Haledjian [hal'ə•djən]

Dr. Haledjian is a brilliant detective. In fact, he's so clever that often he doesn't even need to visit the scene of a crime! Just by listening to what happened, Dr. Haledjian was able to solve these four mysteries. Can you do the same? All the clues you'll need are given. When you think you have the solutions, check them against the doctor's. Then score yourself as a sleuth!

BLACKMAILER

"Inheriting my father's millions has had its nerve-racking moments," said Thomas Hunt to Dr. Haledjian. "Do you remember Martin

Keyes, the gardener?"

"A nasty little chap," answered Haledjian.

"That's right. I dismissed him when I inherited the house in East Hampton. Well, three days ago he came to my office. He wanted $100,000. He claimed that he had been tending the maple trees outside my father's study when he saw Dad draw up another will. That will named my uncle in New Zealand sole heir."

"You believed him?" asked Haledjian.

"I confess the news hit me like a thunderbolt," Hunt answered. "Dad and I had quarreled over Veronica sometime during the last week in November. Dad was against our marriage, and it seemed possible that he had cut me off. Keyes said he possessed this second will. He felt sure it would be worth a good deal more to me than he was asking. The will was dated November 31—the day after the first will. Therefore, Keyes claimed, the second will would be legally recognized.

"I refused to be blackmailed," Hunt continued. "Keyes tried to bargain, asking

$50,000 and then $25,000."

"You paid nothing, I hope?" asked Haledjian.

"Not a penny," answered Hunt.

"You were quite right," approved Haledjian. "Imagine trying to peddle a tale like that!"

What was Keyes's mistake?

THE CASE OF THE LAST MORENO

"From the smirk on your face, I assume you have a new idea for making a million dollars," Dr. Haledjian said to Bertie Tilford.

"Not quite a million," corrected Tilford. He opened his briefcase and showed Haledjian a pen-and-ink drawing of a bearded man.

"It looks like a drawing by the great artist Tassado Moreno!" Haledjian marveled.

"Exactly," gloated Tilford. "All the world knows Moreno died in Alaska three years ago.

The details of his death weren't made known at that time. Then, a few weeks ago, his friend, Kiako,[2] met hard times and came to me.

"The facts are," continued Tilford, "that Moreno had been ill for some time. Then he injured his hip in a storm. His and Kiako's supplies were buried on the trail. The temperature had been far below freezing for days. Moreno's condition rapidly became worse. Kiako got him to an abandoned shack. He stopped up the broken window with his gloves. As he tore apart a chair to build a fire, Moreno called to him. There was no time. He wouldn't live half an hour.

"Moreno asked for drawing materials," Tilford went on. "Kiako found an old pen and a

---

[2]Kiako [kī/ə•kō]

bottle of ink in a cupboard. Moreno sketched his faithful friend, and then he died.

"The prices of Moreno's drawings have soared since his death. His last picture should be worth a quarter of a million dollars. I can buy it from Kiako for $20,000," concluded Tilford. "Have you got the money, old boy?"

"For that portrait? I wouldn't pay 20 cents for it!" snapped Haledjian.

Why wouldn't Haledjian pay anything for the portrait?

THE CASE OF THE
UNKOWN BROTHER

Mrs. Sydney was New York's most famous party-giver. Smiling, she settled back in her dinner chair. She was about to begin her favorite form of entertainment— trying to puzzle the great detective, Dr. Haledjian.

"My childhood playmate, Jedediah[3] Wright, ran away from home when he was 12," she began. "For years he lived by odd jobs. But in 1927, he settled in Michigan and

---

[3]Jedediah [jed/ə•dī/ə]

made millions in copper. Unfortunately Jed never married. On his deathbed he called his faithful housekeeper and handed her a fat envelope containing cash, deeds, and securities.

"His parents had passed away ten years earlier," Mrs. Sydney went on. "Jed's only living relative was a brother. 'Give this envelope to my brother, Alf,' the dying man told the housekeeper. The housekeeper had never seen Alf in her life. Her only clue was a yellowed photograph set in a double frame with one of Jed. The pictures had been taken 55 years before, on their tenth birthday. Also, the housekeeper had only one clue to Alf's whereabouts. That was a letter postmarked the month before from Los Angeles."

Mrs. Sydney paused

and smiled at Dr. Haledjian. "The housekeeper went to Los Angeles and advertised the reason for her visit," she continued. "Soon 100 men were camped outside her hotel door. She had never seen Alf and knew nothing about him. Yet she was able to pick him out of the crowd of impostors!"

"My dear Mrs. Sydney, to what ends will you go to stump an old sleuth?" said Haledjian with a reproachful sigh. "The answer is elementary."

How did the housekeeper know Alf?

23

THE CASE OF THE
STOLEN JEWELS

Mrs. Sydney had never satisfied her fondest desire. This was to baffle the master sleuth, Dr. Haledjian.

That was why Haledjian was on his guard when, after dinner, Mrs. Sydney leaned back in her chair and told him about the frightening experience she had had the night before.

"You will hardly believe how close I came to losing my life and my jewels last night," she began. "It must have been around 3:00 A.M. when a noise woke me. A masked man was standing in my room. By the moonlight, I could see two more men climbing through the open window."

Mrs. Sydney shuddered at the memory and went on. "I was tied up and gagged. Then the men went through my jewels. Helpless, I watched them fill a sack with gems. I was afraid they would kill me if I did anything. Finally they finished and started out the window.

"As the last of them went out, I screamed for help," Mrs. Sydney continued. "Patrolman Casey was a block away and heard me. The men dropped the sack in their hurry to escape from him, so my jewels are safe. However, it will take me a month to recover from the scare."

Dr. Haledjian smiled.

"My dear Mrs. Sydney," he said, "your recovery from an experience that never happened will certainly be short."

What was wrong with Mrs. Sydney's story?

SOLUTIONS

THE CASE OF THE
BLACKMAILER

No legal will could be dated November 31. November has only 30 days.

THE CASE OF THE
UNKOWN BROTHER

The housekeeper knew Alf through her one clue—the photograph. It had been taken "55 years before, on their tenth birthday." Alf and Jed were identical twins!

THE CASE OF THE
LAST MORENO

Tilford said that "the temperature had been far below freezing for days" and the shack had a "broken window." In these conditions Moreno couldn't have made a pen-and-ink drawing of Kiako because the ink would have been frozen solid.

THE CASE OF THE
STOLEN JEWELS

Mrs. Sydney said she was "helpless," having been tied up and "gagged." Therefore, it would have been impossible for her to cry out loudly enough for Patrolman Casey to have heard her from "a block away."

Talk about it!

1 After reading these mysteries, do you think you would make a good detective?

2 When did you first know the solution to each mystery?

3 Retell each mystery in three or four sentences.

4 Which of the four mysteries do you think was the easiest to solve? Explain your answer.

5 Paying attention to details can help detectives solve mysteries. What other kinds of problems can be solved by paying attention to details?

Bibliography

The House of Dies Drear *by Virginia Hamilton. Macmillan.* The mystery of an enormous old house, once a station on the Underground Railway, is revealed in this exciting book.

Mark Twain Murders *by Laurence Yep. Scholastic.* Mark Twain and a fifteen-year-old boy uncover a plot that threatens their lives.

The Puzzler *(microcomputer program). Sunburst.* Takes you through five mini-mysteries in search of clues.

DRAFTER OF DREAMS

by Beatrice Julian and Jesse Palm

Lewis Latimer dreamed of doing something important. With his inventive talent and hard work, he drafted a place in American history.

29

A chill wind blew through the city of Boston. A young African-American boy stood on a street corner with a stack of newspapers under one arm. Now and then he rushed after some figure in the gathering twilight, calling out, "Paper, sir? Paper?"

Lewis Howard Latimer was ten years old in that winter of 1859. His childhood, however, had already ended. It had ended on that dreadful day some months back when his father disappeared. Because Lewis's father had been a slave, some said George Latimer's former owner caught him. He may have been taken back to the Southern plantation from which he had escaped 19 years before. No one really knew. To little Lewis, only one thing seemed certain. His family was in trouble, and he had to do his part to save it.

The darkness thickened. A man went by with a torch to light the gas street lamps. Rows of lampposts flickered to life like spindly yellow flowers. They shed only a poor light. Errand boys darted like shadows through the crowd. They were carrying messages from office to office, for telephones had not been invented yet. Neither had cars. In the crowded street, horses snorted and carriage wheels squeaked.

"Paper, sir . . . ?"

Lewis stumbled after one last possible customer. The man scarcely glanced at Lewis. Wrapped in his own important thoughts, he strode away. Lewis stared after him for some moments. Then he tucked the remaining papers under his shirt and started home.

Here and there in the towering ten-story buildings around him, windows were lighting up. Important people were up there doing important work, no doubt. Lewis's head drooped. How he longed to be a part of all that excitement and bustle! How he longed to do something important! The chances, however, seemed remote. Never had the world seemed so huge. Never had Lewis felt so small.

Twelve years later, Lewis Latimer sat behind a desk in a tall building in Boston. Much had happened in those years. The Civil War had cracked the United States in half. Enormous armies had clashed in some of history's bloodiest battles. In the third year of the war, Latimer had joined the navy and seen action as a cabin boy on the *U.S.S. Massasoit*. He had played his small part unnoticed in the war that ended slavery. Afterwards he returned to Boston to look for work, but so did thousands of other hungry veterans. Latimer felt lucky to get a job as an errand boy. He went to work for the law firm of Crosby and Gould.

Latimer was luckier than he knew. America had just entered the golden age of invention. Within 50 years a flood of ingenious new devices would transform the nation. Crosby and Gould worked exclusively with inventors. They processed patents, documents that gave inventors legal ownership of their designs. Working for this firm put Latimer in the thick of the greatest drama of his time.

Lewis was ambitious. When the drudgery of running errands wore thin, he looked around for another job in the firm. The one that caught his eye was drafting.

At the law firm Latimer had watched the patent draftsmen make accurate drawings of inventions. Their drawings showed how the inventions worked. The job took precision and technical knowledge. The draftsmen had to understand the inventions they were drawing.

Latimer was no engineer. His schooling had been spotty. Whatever he knew, he had taught to himself. Fortunately, he had been an excellent teacher and student. He now set to work to teach himself drafting. He studied at night, using secondhand tools. Some of the draftsmen in the law firm gave him advice. When he showed samples of his work to his employers, they were astounded. They wasted no time promoting Lewis Latimer from errand boy to draftsman.

Thus it happened that Latimer was in the office the day the gentleman with muttonchop whiskers came in. Lewis knew the man. His name was Alexander Graham Bell. He ran a school for the deaf nearby. Lewis had chatted with him in the street a few times.

Lewis knew that Bell liked to tinker. People said Bell was working on some sort of invention. In 1876 this did not make Bell very special. Practically everybody liked to tinker in those days. Inventing was a popular hobby, much like "computer hacking" in recent times. Thousands of amateur inventors dreamed of getting lucky. They dreamed of stumbling across some great invention that would make them rich.

Bell looked slightly embarrassed when he entered the office. He nodded to Lewis and then went to the

gray-haired Mr. Crosby. The two men spoke in low tones for a few minutes. Then they approached Lewis Latimer.

Mr. Crosby said that Bell had invented something. He needed a good draftsman. "I have recommended that he give the job to you."

Lewis nodded. He went with Bell to look at the invention. On the way he sensed Bell's excitement. He followed Bell into a small room. Wires and tools lay heaped in the corners. On a table in the middle of the room sat what looked like a metal ice cream cone turned on its side. Next to the cone was a small coil of wires. The whole assembly was supported by columns on a wooden base with two wires connected to it. One of the wires ran from the bottom of the device and out the door.

Bell asked Lewis to sit down in front of the device and pointed to the cone. Latimer noticed that Bell's fingers were trembling slightly. "Listen closely," Bell said. Then he left the room.

Latimer sat forward and waited. Suddenly a voice came from the strange device, startling him. He could not make out the words, but the sound was definitely that of a human voice. Latimer knew then that Bell was not just tinkering. He was working on one of the great inventions of history.

Bell's invention was, of course, the telephone. Latimer drafted the plans and helped Bell get his patent. In the years that followed, Latimer became more interested in inventing. Before he met Bell, he had already invented a few gadgets of his own. Now his creative imagination seemed to catch fire.

In 1880 Latimer went to work for Hiram Maxim, who invented the machine gun. Maxim now headed the U.S. Electric Lighting Company. One year earlier Thomas Edison had invented the electric light bulb. Latimer set to work to invent a better one.

The trouble with Edison's light bulb was the filament. This was the little thread that glowed inside the bulb. Edison's filament burned too quickly. Latimer invented one that cost less to make and lasted much longer. Within a few years, Latimer's bulbs came into use in railroad stations all across the United States and Canada.

Latimer's inventive talents soon caught Thomas Edison's attention. Edison hired him, and the two men worked together for many years. Latimer helped improve Edison's electrical devices and explained Edison's work to the public in books and in speeches. His work earned him membership in the "Edison Pioneers," a select group of scientists who had worked with Edison.

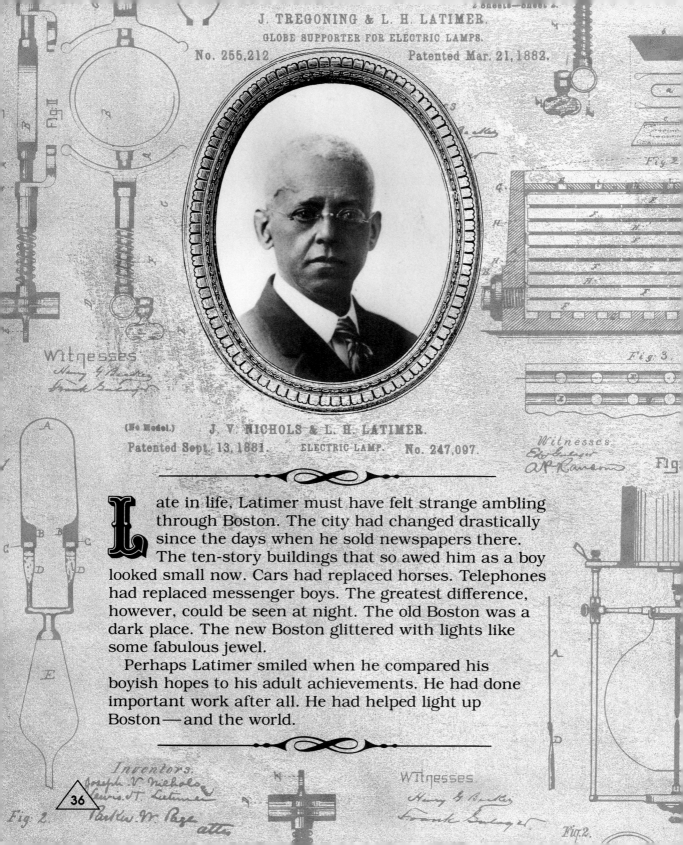

J. TREGONING & L. H. LATIMER.

GLOBE SUPPORTER FOR ELECTRIC LAMPS.

No. 255,212   Patented Mar. 21, 1882.

(No Model.)   J. V. NICHOLS & L. H. LATIMER.

Patented Sept. 13, 1881.   ELECTRIC LAMP.   No. 247,097.

Late in life, Latimer must have felt strange ambling through Boston. The city had changed drastically since the days when he sold newspapers there. The ten-story buildings that so awed him as a boy looked small now. Cars had replaced horses. Telephones had replaced messenger boys. The greatest difference, however, could be seen at night. The old Boston was a dark place. The new Boston glittered with lights like some fabulous jewel.

Perhaps Latimer smiled when he compared his boyish hopes to his adult achievements. He had done important work after all. He had helped light up Boston—and the world.

L. H.
PROCESS OF
No. 252,386.

LATIMER.
MANUFACTURING CARBONS.
Patented Jan. 17, 188

Talk about it!

1 What place in American history did Lewis Latimer draft for himself?

2 What were some of Lewis Latimer's achievements?

3 How did you feel about Lewis at the beginning of the selection? Did your feelings about him change by the end of the selection? Explain your answer.

4 Why do you think the author begins the story by telling about Lewis at age ten?

5 What does the author want us to learn by reading about Lewis Latimer's life?

Bibliography

Encyclopedia of Black America edited by W. Augustus Low. McGraw-Hill. Several hundred biographies of African Americans and essays about black history and life make this an important resource.

Weird and Wacky Inventions by Jim Murphy. Crown. Some of the strangest inventions ever patented are shown and described in this book.

Turn of the Century America (videocassette). Guidance Associates. Takes you back to the time when Lewis Latimer's inventions were coming into use.

My Uncle Dan

by Ted Hughes

My Uncle Dan's an inventor. You may think that's very fine.
You may wish he were your uncle instead of being mine—
If he wanted he could make a watch that bounces when it drops,
He could make a helicopter out of string and bottle tops
Or any really useful thing you can't get in the shops.
   But Uncle Dan has other ideas:
   The bottomless glass for ginger beers,
   The toothless saw that's safe for the tree,
   A special word for a spelling bee
   (Like Lionocerangoutangadder),
   Or the roll-uppable rubber ladder,
   The mystery pie that bites when it's bit—
   My Uncle Dan invented it.
My Uncle Dan sits in his den inventing night and day.
His eyes peer from his hair and beard like mice from a load of hay.
And does he make the shoes that will go for walks without your feet?
A shrinker to shrink instantly the elephants you meet?
A carver that just from the air carves steaks cooked and ready to eat?
   No, no, he has other intentions—
   Only perfectly useless inventions:
   Glassless windows (they never break),
   A medicine to cure the earthquake,
   The unspillable screwed-down cup,
   The stairs that go neither down nor up
   The door you simply paint on a wall—
   Uncle Dan invented them all.

Goose BUMPS and FUNNY BONES

from the MACMILLAN ILLUSTRATED
ALMANAC FOR KIDS
by Ann Elwood and Carol Orsag

Have you ever wondered why some people have dimples or how you get goose bumps? Here are the answers to these and other questions about the amazing human body.

How do you get goose bumps?

Each hair on your body grows in its own shaft, called a follicle. If you feel cold or afraid, the smooth muscles around the follicles contract, giving you goose bumps and making the hairs stand upright.

What makes your knuckles crack?

A fluid surrounds the joints of your finger bones. When you stretch your fingers, the pressure on the fluid changes and little bubbles form in the fluid. The sound of these bubbles popping is the crack of your knuckles! If you want to crack the same knuckles again, you have to wait about 15 minutes.

How long does an eyelash live?

An eyelash lives about 150 days.

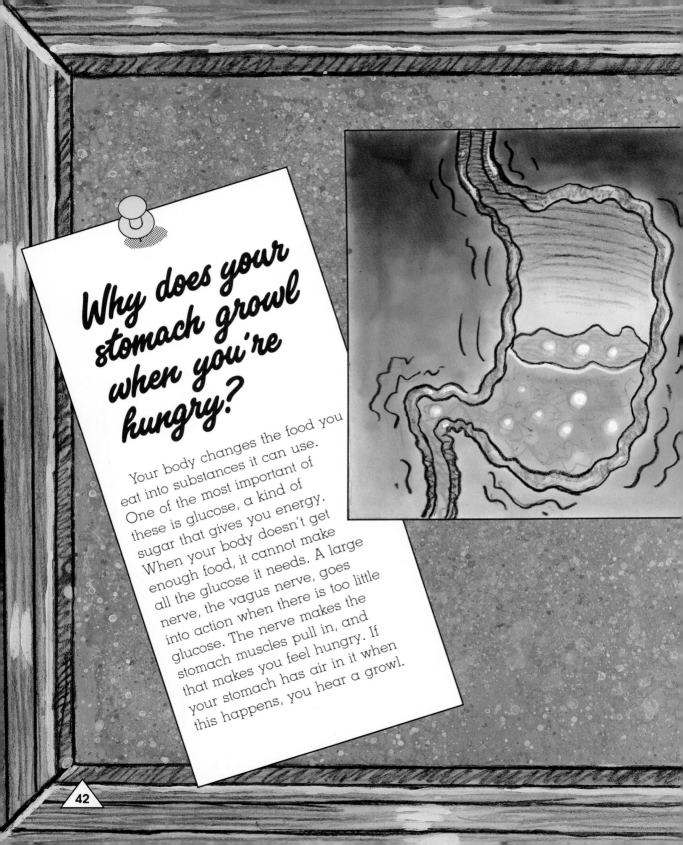

Why does your stomach growl when you're hungry?

Your body changes the food you eat into substances it can use. One of the most important of these is glucose, a kind of sugar that gives you energy. When your body doesn't get enough food, it cannot make all the glucose it needs. A large nerve, the vagus nerve, goes into action when there is too little glucose. The nerve makes the stomach muscles pull in, and that makes you feel hungry. If your stomach has air in it when this happens, you hear a growl.

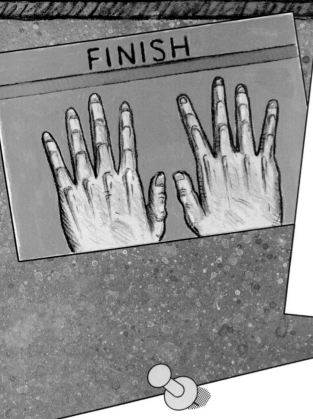

FINISH

How fast do your fingernails grow?

The average amount of fingernail growth is 1/25 of an inch a week. Fingernails grow faster on the hand you use the most. If you're right-handed, your right fingernails grow faster; if you're left-handed, your left fingernails grow faster.

How many muscles does it take to smile?

It takes 17 muscles to smile. You use 43 muscles when you frown.

What is the funny bone?

The term *funny bone* comes from the real name of a particular bone in your elbow, the *humerus*. (Do you understand the joke?) A big nerve rests against this bone, just underneath the skin. If you strike that nerve against something hard, the sensation may be funny in the sense of being peculiar, but it certainly won't make you laugh!

HA HA
TEE HEE HA HA

When are people the healthiest?

People are healthiest between the ages of 5 and 15.

When do kids stop growing?

Boys have achieved 98 percent of their height when they reach the age of 17 3/4 years. Girls have reached 98 percent of their height by the time they are 16 1/2 years old.

How many sounds can you hear?

You can hear between 350,000 and 400,000 different sounds.

Why do some people have dimples?

Dimples are caused by muscles in the face. Most muscles in the body are attached to bones, but the muscles that cause dimples are attached to the skin. The movement of these muscles when a person smiles causes the dimples to form.

When is your eye still?

Your eyes are never still. They move continuously, even when you're staring at something. The tiny muscles in the eyes move about 100,000 times a day to let you see. For your leg muscles to get the same amount of exercise as your eye muscles, you would have to walk 50 miles.

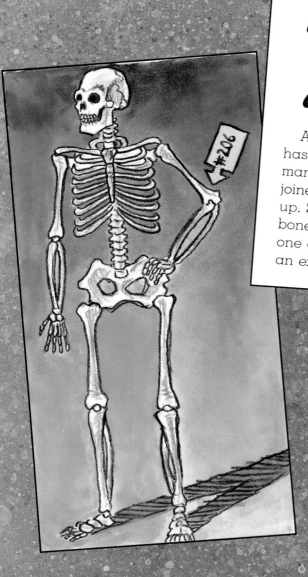

#206

How many bones do you have in your body?

A baby has 330 bones. An adult has only 206 bones. This is because many of the baby's bones have joined together by the time it grows up. Some people have an extra bone in the arch of their foot. Also, one out of every 20 people has an extra rib.

Are kids today taller than kids who lived 100 years ago?

Kids today are taller by about six inches than kids who lived 100 years ago.

Why do people have either straight, wavy, or curly hair?

The degree or lack of curl all depends on the shape of the hair follicle. People with round follicles have straight hair. People with oval follicles have wavy hair, and those with slit-shaped follicles have curly hair.

How fast does your hair grow?

Hair on your head grows about one-hundredth of an inch a day. As you get older, it grows a little more slowly. You have about 100,000 hairs on your head, and each one lives from two to four years. During an average lifetime, hair on your head grows about 25 feet.

How much air do the lungs use in one day?

Lungs use about 12,500 quarts of air in one day.

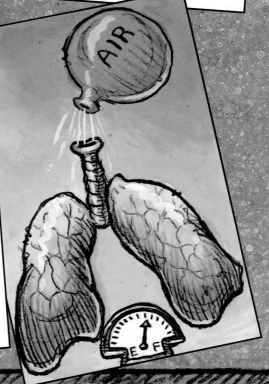

How long can you live without water?

You can live only about ten days without water, because 60 percent of your body is water.

How many different smells can humans smell?

The average person knows 4,000 different smells. Some people with a very special sense of smell know 10,000 different scents! People who test perfumes have this special talent.

Talk about it!

1 Which facts about the human body did you find most amazing?

2 Suppose a friend asked you to explain what this selection is about. How would you summarize the selection in two or three sentences?

3 Reread the subheadings. What do they tell you about the selection?

Bibliography

Body Sense/Body Nonsense by Seymour Simon. Little, Brown. Little-known facts and common misconceptions about the body are discussed in this lively book.

Macmillan Book of the Human Body by Mary Elting. Macmillan. Large diagrams and illustrations give detailed information about the body and how it works.

Human Body: An Overview (microcomputer program). Brain-Bank. Presents and reviews body systems in a lively manner.

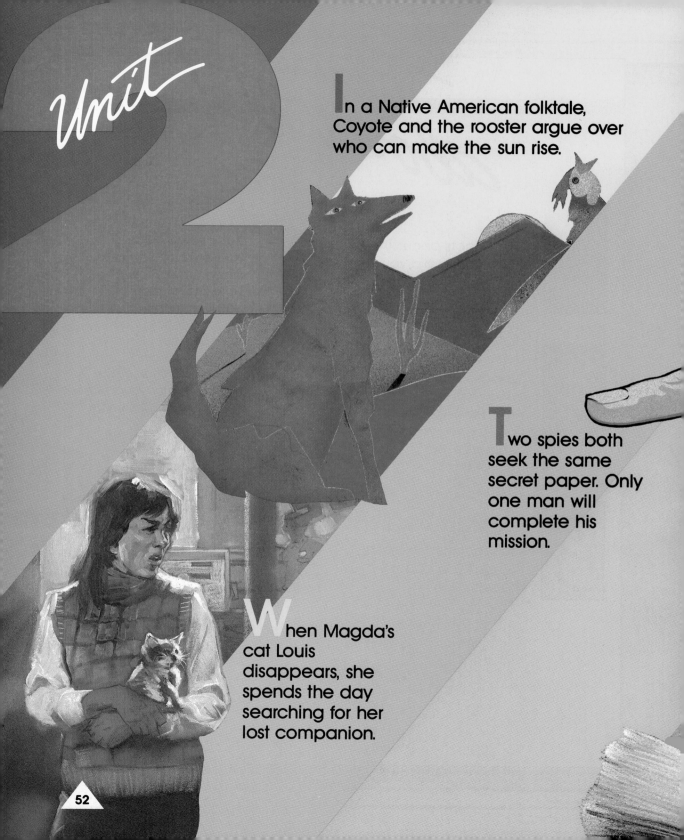

Unit 2

In a Native American folktale, Coyote and the rooster argue over who can make the sun rise.

Two spies both seek the same secret paper. Only one man will complete his mission.

When Magda's cat Louis disappears, she spends the day searching for her lost companion.

Read about five American cities that are full of fun things to do and see.

Find out how American spies managed to fool the enemy during World War II.

Discover what your thumbprint says about you.

A BAD ROAD FOR CATS

from EVERY LIVING THING

by Cynthia Rylant

Louis was missing and the
woman was worried. Route 6
was a bad road for cats.
Would she find him?

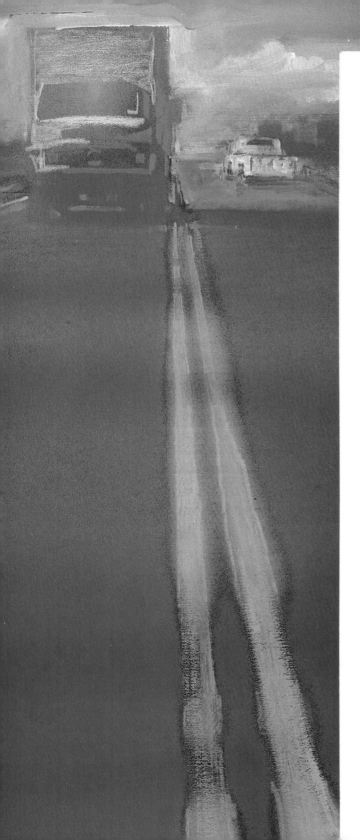

"LOUIE! LOUIS! Where are you?"

The woman called it out again and again as she walked along Route 6. A bad road for cats. She prayed he hadn't wandered this far. But it had been nearly two weeks, and still Louis hadn't come home.

She stopped at a gas station, striding up to the young man at the register. Her eyes snapped black and fiery as she spit the question at him: "Have you seen a *cat*?" The word *cat* came out hard as a rock.

The young man straightened up. "No, ma'am. No cats around here."

The woman's eyes pinched his. "I lost my cat. Orange and white. If you see him, you be careful with him. This is a bad road for cats." She marched toward the door. "I'll be back," she said, like a threat, and the young man straightened up again as she went out.

"Louie! Louis! Where are you?"

She was a very tall woman, and skinny. Her black hair was long and shiny, like a Native American's. She might have been a Cherokee making her way alongside a river, alert and watchful. Tracking.

But Route 6 was no river. It was a truckers' road, lined with gas stations, motels, dairy bars, and diners. A nasty road, smelling of diesel and rubber.

The woman's name was Magda. And she was of French blood, not Indian. She lived in a small house about two miles off Route 6. There she worked at a loom, using yarn made from the wool of the sheep she owned. Magda's husband was dead, and she had no children. Only a cat named Louis.

Dunh. Dunh. Duuunnh.

Magda's heart pounded as a tank truck roared by. *Duuunnh.* The horn hurt her ears, making her feel sick inside, stealing some of her strength.

Four years before, Magda had found Louis at one of the gas stations on Route 6. She had been on her way home from her weekly trip to the grocery and had pulled in for a fill-up. Standing inside the station she'd felt warm fur against her leg and had given a start. Looking down, she'd seen an orange-and-white kitten. It had purred and meowed and pushed its nose into Magda's shoes. Smiling, Magda had picked up the kitten. Then she had seen the horror.

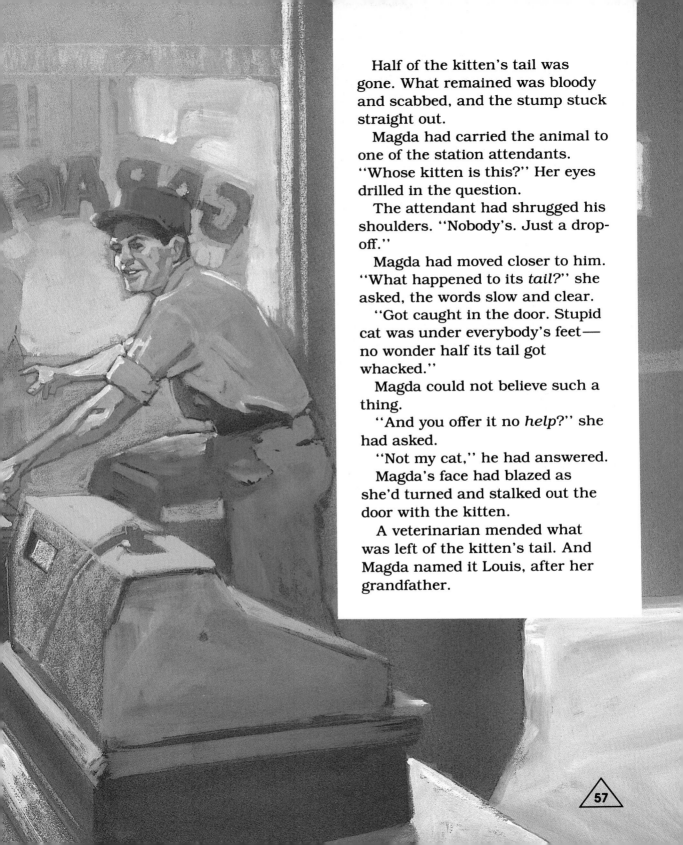

Half of the kitten's tail was gone. What remained was bloody and scabbed, and the stump stuck straight out.

Magda had carried the animal to one of the station attendants. "Whose kitten is this?" Her eyes drilled in the question.

The attendant had shrugged his shoulders. "Nobody's. Just a drop-off."

Magda had moved closer to him. "What happened to its *tail?*" she asked, the words slow and clear.

"Got caught in the door. Stupid cat was under everybody's feet— no wonder half its tail got whacked."

Magda could not believe such a thing.

"And you offer it no *help?*" she had asked.

"Not my cat," he had answered.

Magda's face had blazed as she'd turned and stalked out the door with the kitten.

A veterinarian mended what was left of the kitten's tail. And Magda named it Louis, after her grandfather.

"Louie! Louis! Where are you?"

Magda saw a dairy bar up ahead. She thought she would stop and rest. She would have something to drink and a slice of quiet away from the road.

Magda barely glanced at the young girl working inside. All teenage girls looked alike to her.

"Orange juice," she ordered.

"Ice?"

"Yes."

Magda moved to one side and leaned against the building. The trucks were rolling out on the highway, but far enough away to give her time to regain her strength. No horns, no smoke, no dirt. A little peace.

She drank her juice and thought about Louis when he was a kitten. Once, he had leaped from her attic window, and she had found him, stunned and shivering, on the hard gravel below. The veterinarian said Louis had broken a leg and was lucky to be alive. The kitten had stomped around in a cast for a few weeks. Magda drew funny faces on it to cheer him up.

Louis loved white cheese, tall grass, and the skeins of yarn Magda left lying around her loom.

That's what she would miss most, she thought, if Louis never came back: an orange-and-white cat making the yarn fly under her loom.

Magda finished her juice, then turned to throw the empty cup into the trash can. As she did, a little sign in the bottom corner of the window caught her eye. The words were surrounded by dirty smudges.

4 Sal
CAT

Magda caught her breath. She moved up to the window and this time looked squarely into the face of the girl.

"Are you selling a *cat*?" she said quietly, but quite hard on *cat*.

"Not me. This boy," the girl answered, brushing her stringy hair back from her face.

"Where is he?" Magda asked.

"That yellow house right off the road up there."

Magda headed across the lot.

She had to knock only once. The door opened, and standing there was a boy about fifteen.

"I saw your sign," Magda said. "I am interested in your cat."

The boy did not answer. He looked at Magda's face with his wide blue eyes and he grinned, showing a mouth of rotten and missing teeth.

Magda felt a chill move over her.

"The cat," she repeated. "You have one to sell? Is it orange and white?"

The boy stopped grinning. Without a word, he slammed the door in Magda's face.

She was stunned. A strong woman like her, to be so stunned by a boy. It shamed her. But again she knocked on the door— and very hard this time. No answer.

"What kind of boy is this?" Magda asked herself. A strange one. And she feared he had Louis.

She had just raised her hand to knock a third time when the door opened. There the boy stood with Louis in his arms.

Again, Magda was stunned. Her cat was covered with oil and dirt. He was thin, and his head hung weakly. When he saw Magda, he seemed to use his last bit of strength to let go a pleading cry.

The boy no longer was grinning. He held Louis close against him, forcefully stroking the cat's ears again and again and again. The boy's eyes were full of tears, his mouth twisted into sad protest.

Magda wanted to leap for Louis, steal him, and run for home. But she knew better. This was an unusual boy. She must be careful.

Magda put her hand into her pocket and pulled out a dollar bill.

"Enough?" she asked, holding it up.

The boy clutched the cat harder, his mouth puckering fiercely.

Magda pulled out two more dollar bills. She held the money up, the question in her eyes.

The boy relaxed his hold on Louis. He tilted his head to one side, as if considering Magda's offer.

Then, in desperation, Magda pulled out a twenty-dollar bill.

"*Enough?*" she almost screamed.

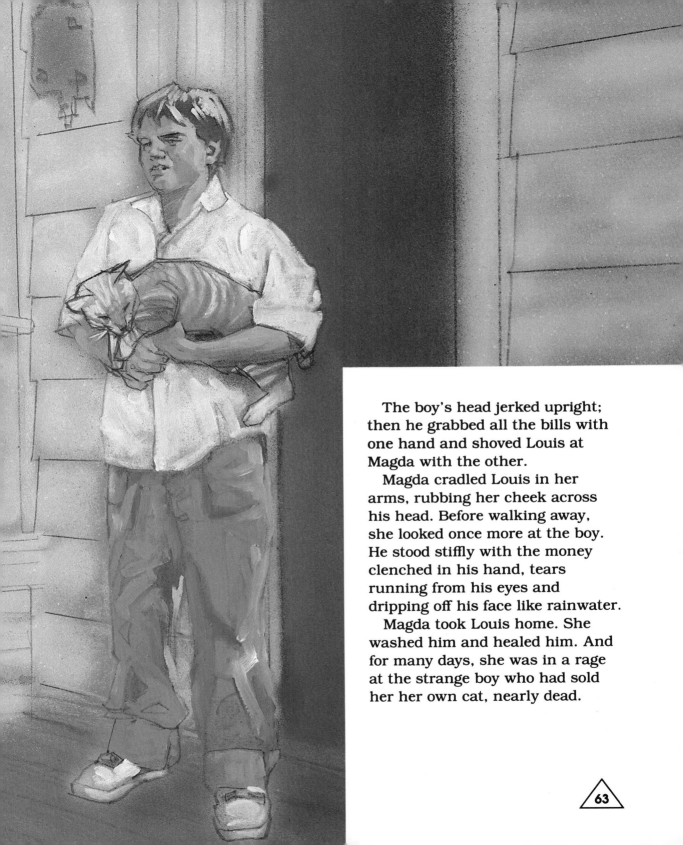

The boy's head jerked upright;
then he grabbed all the bills with
one hand and shoved Louis at
Magda with the other.

Magda cradled Louis in her
arms, rubbing her cheek across
his head. Before walking away,
she looked once more at the boy.
He stood stiffly with the money
clenched in his hand, tears
running from his eyes and
dripping off his face like rainwater.

Magda took Louis home. She
washed him and healed him. And
for many days, she was in a rage
at the strange boy who had sold
her her own cat, nearly dead.

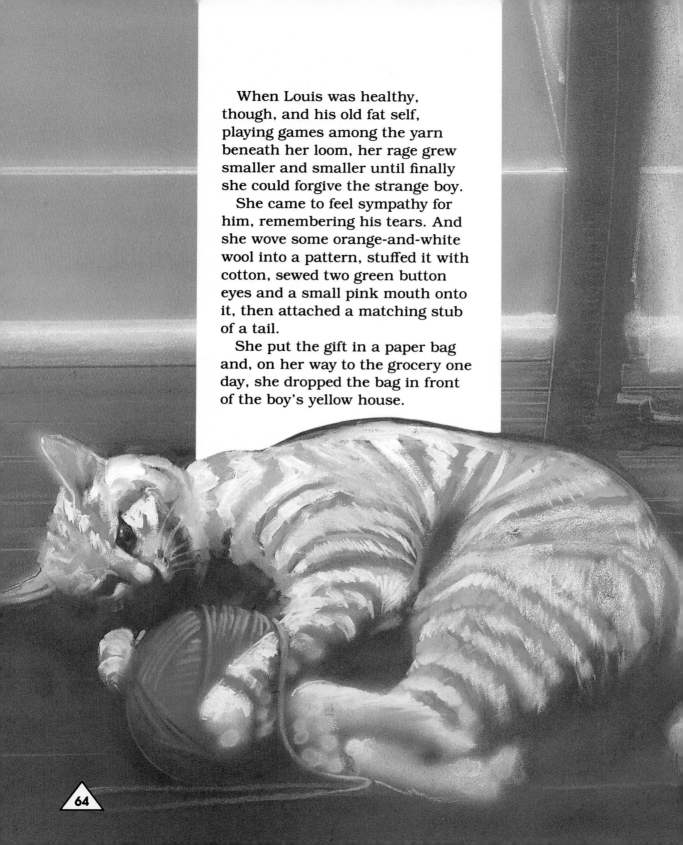

When Louis was healthy, though, and his old fat self, playing games among the yarn beneath her loom, her rage grew smaller and smaller until finally she could forgive the strange boy.

She came to feel sympathy for him, remembering his tears. And she wove some orange-and-white wool into a pattern, stuffed it with cotton, sewed two green button eyes and a small pink mouth onto it, then attached a matching stub of a tail.

She put the gift in a paper bag and, on her way to the grocery one day, she dropped the bag in front of the boy's yellow house.

Talk about it!

1 How does Magda find Louis?

2 On pages 56 and 57 the writer interrupts the present action of the story to tell you about Magda and Louis. What do you learn about them?

3 Magda says that the boy is strange. How does the writer "show" that this is true? Read aloud the lines.

4 How do you feel about the boy? Would you have forgiven him, as Magda did? Explain your answer.

5 How does the saying "You can't judge a book by its cover" apply to Magda?

Bibliography

The Cat Who Went to Heaven by Elizabeth Coatsworth. Macmillan. This classic story tells of a Japanese artist and his cat, named Good Fortune.

One-Eyed Cat by Paula Fox. Bradbury. Ned cares for a stray cat that he believes he has accidentally wounded.

Cats (videocassette). Lucerne. Explores the reasons why people have loved cats throughout history.

THE *Secrets* OF THE SECRET AGENTS

by Michael Di Leo

Prison or death was the danger these agents faced. The smallest mistake could reveal who they really were. How did they manage to fool the enemy?

Aramis

During World War II, a man called Aramis roamed the streets of Paris carrying an easel, tubes of paint, and some brushes. He seemed to spend all his days painting pictures of the lovely bridges that crossed the Seine River in the middle of the city.

At that time, France was occupied by Germany. The German secret police, the Gestapo, were always on the alert for spies and secret agents in Paris. The Gestapo ignored Aramis, figuring he was harmless, but they were wrong. Had they investigated, they would have discovered that Aramis never sold a single painting. Where, then, did he get the money he needed to live?

In fact, Aramis was a secret agent. Instead of painting bridges, he was drawing fortifications the Germans had placed along the Seine. His drawings served as reports to American generals who were planning an invasion of France. Aramis also acted as a lookout when other agents sabotaged German operations. As it turned out for the Germans, Aramis was anything but harmless.

How did Aramis fool the Gestapo for so long? The secret was his "cover." He looked and acted just like a French painter. His accent, his clothing, and his identification papers all fit perfectly the character he played.

THE Clothing
OF OSS AGENTS

Aramis was part of one of the most successful espionage groups in history. This group, the Office of Strategic Services, or OSS, was formed by the United States government during World War II. At its peak, the OSS had about 12,000 men and women serving as secret agents throughout the world.

Before going into the field, OSS agents reported to a plain-looking building in the center of London. This was the clothing and documents section of the OSS. Here were a tailor, a shoemaker, and experts in printing, paper, and cloth. They all worked to make sure that an agent's "cover" was fully convincing.

The OSS workers knew that every detail of an agent's appearance could be a matter of life and death. Even the thread in a button could give an agent away. In England and America, the thread in four-holed buttons ran vertically. The person who attached them to a piece of clothing first passed the thread through the two holes on the left. Then he or she passed the thread through the two holes on the right. Most agents, however, were stationed in France. In that country, the thread in four-holed buttons ran in crisscross style. Every button on every garment to be worn by an agent in France had to be attached in the French fashion.

After agents had received all the right clothes, they were sent to a dentist. At that time, dentists in the United States used gold to fill cavities. In France, however, dentists used silver. One smile could give an agent away and tip off the Gestapo. All agents were ordered to have all their gold dental work replaced with silver. This process, though unpleasant, kept many a spy from being discovered.

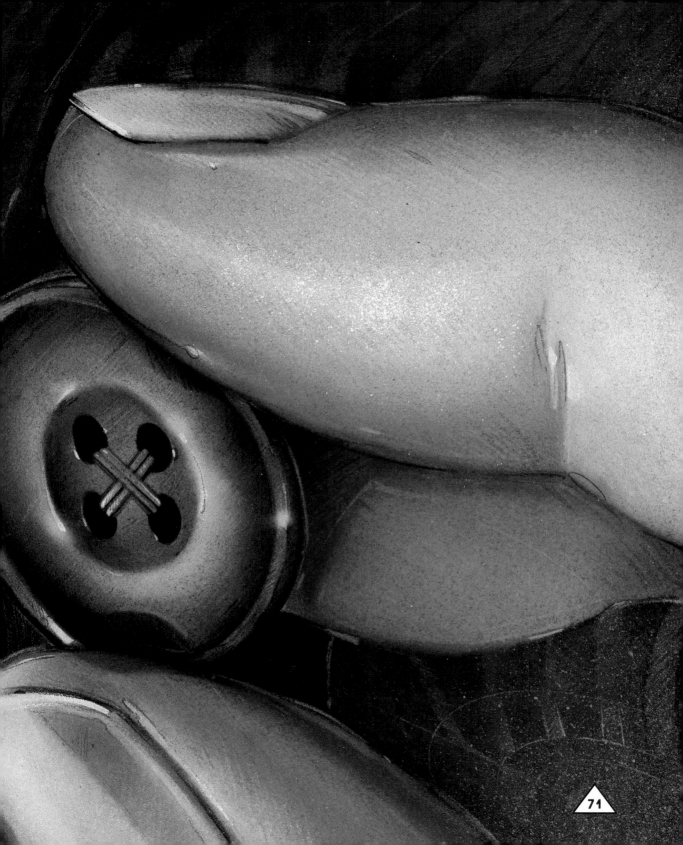

THE OSS
Documents

Just as important as the tailor and dentist were the OSS document workers. During World War II, every person in Europe carried an identity card. The Gestapo often checked people's cards to find secret agents. To protect agents, the OSS developed ways of making exact copies of identity cards. These copies were made from the same paper and ink and used the same style of type as the real cards.

Real identity cards were usually well worn from use. A new-looking card might have aroused suspicion. Therefore, the false cards were made to look old by the document workers. First the cards were rubbed in ashes or a powder made of crushed rock. Then the corners of the cards were carefully rounded off with sandpaper. As a last touch, OSS workers carried the cards around in their pockets for weeks at a time until the papers were stained with sweat. By the time an agent received a false card, it always looked as if it had been used for months or even years.

Knowing that OSS agents were carrying false documents, the Germans added a nine-digit number to all French identity cards. The OSS soon learned about the new number. They then added a nine-digit number to the false cards. Something went wrong, however. All agents showing the new cards were quickly arrested.

The OSS workers were puzzled. How, they wondered, could the Germans tell false OSS cards from real ones? OSS workers realized that the answer lay with the new nine-digit numbers. Those numbers were a code designed by the Germans. Before long, OSS experts had figured out the code.

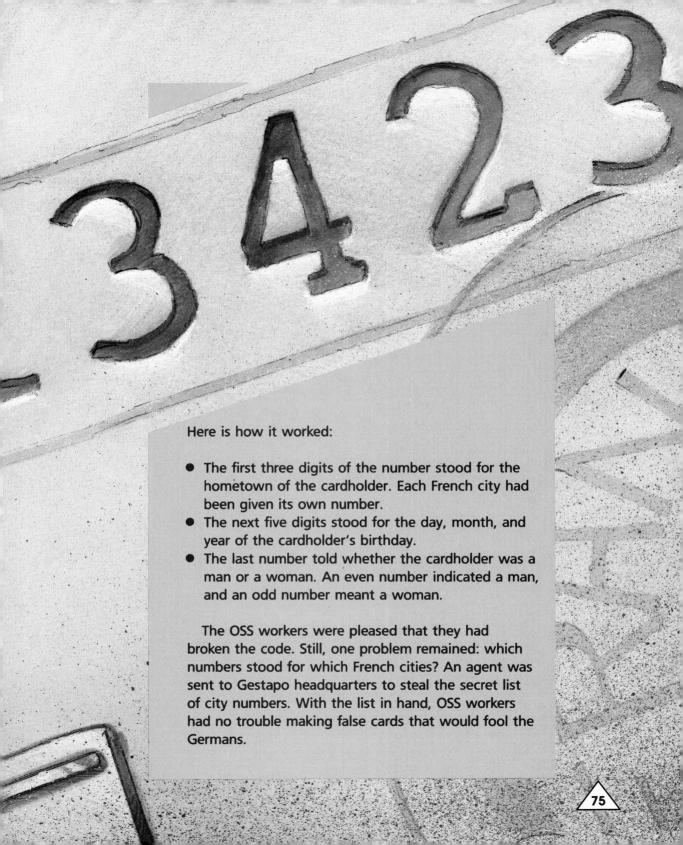

Here is how it worked:

- The first three digits of the number stood for the hometown of the cardholder. Each French city had been given its own number.
- The next five digits stood for the day, month, and year of the cardholder's birthday.
- The last number told whether the cardholder was a man or a woman. An even number indicated a man, and an odd number meant a woman.

The OSS workers were pleased that they had broken the code. Still, one problem remained: which numbers stood for which French cities? An agent was sent to Gestapo headquarters to steal the secret list of city numbers. With the list in hand, OSS workers had no trouble making false cards that would fool the Germans.

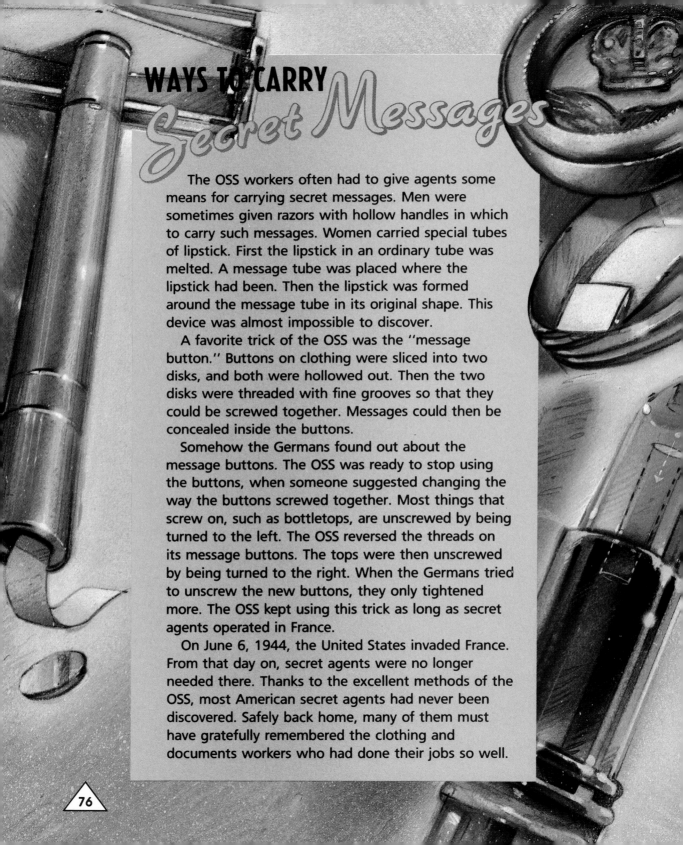

WAYS TO CARRY
Secret Messages

The OSS workers often had to give agents some means for carrying secret messages. Men were sometimes given razors with hollow handles in which to carry such messages. Women carried special tubes of lipstick. First the lipstick in an ordinary tube was melted. A message tube was placed where the lipstick had been. Then the lipstick was formed around the message tube in its original shape. This device was almost impossible to discover.

A favorite trick of the OSS was the "message button." Buttons on clothing were sliced into two disks, and both were hollowed out. Then the two disks were threaded with fine grooves so that they could be screwed together. Messages could then be concealed inside the buttons.

Somehow the Germans found out about the message buttons. The OSS was ready to stop using the buttons, when someone suggested changing the way the buttons screwed together. Most things that screw on, such as bottletops, are unscrewed by being turned to the left. The OSS reversed the threads on its message buttons. The tops were then unscrewed by being turned to the right. When the Germans tried to unscrew the new buttons, they only tightened more. The OSS kept using this trick as long as secret agents operated in France.

On June 6, 1944, the United States invaded France. From that day on, secret agents were no longer needed there. Thanks to the excellent methods of the OSS, most American secret agents had never been discovered. Safely back home, many of them must have gratefully remembered the clothing and documents workers who had done their jobs so well.

Talk about it!

1 How were the secret agents able to fool the enemy?

2 Which secret did you find most interesting?

3 Explain why the secret agents owed much of their success to the efforts of the OSS workers.

4 What new understandings or insights do you have about secret agents and their jobs from reading the selection?

5 Most of the selection describes the OSS and its work. However, the writer begins the selection by describing Aramis. Why does he begin with a description of a person?

Bibliography

Sinister Touches; The Secret War Against Hitler by Robert Goldston. Dial. Brief accounts of the contributions of spies to the Allied victory in World War II.

Behind Enemy Lines by Milton J. Shapiro. Messner. The complete history of the OSS is told in this book about American spies.

A World at War (videocassette). Coronet. Shows how Americans prepared for World War II and how the war was ended in 1945.

78

THUMBPRINT

by Eve Merriam

In the heel of my thumb
are whorls, whirls, wheels
in a unique design:
mine alone.
What a treasure to own!
My own flesh, my own feelings.
No other, however grand or base,
can ever contain the same.
My signature,
thumbing the pages of my time.
My universe key,
my singularity.
Impress, implant,
I am myself,
of all my atom parts I am the sum.
And out of my blood and my brain
I make my own interior weather,
my own sun and rain.
Imprint my mark upon the world,
whatever I shall become.

THE MIDNIGHT VISITOR

by Roger Rittner

Based on the story by
Robert Arthur

Rita Fowler went to Paris to interview a real-life spy. She certainly expected someone more exciting than Howard Austin. The only word that seemed to fit Mr. Austin was *dull*, or so Rita thought—until she met the Midnight Visitor!

Cast of CHARACTERS

Howard **AUSTIN,**	an American espionage agent
Rita **FOWLER,**	an American journalist
Max **KOVSKY,**	a foreign agent
Marie	a waitress
Henri	a night custodian

Narrator: In a small restaurant on the outskirts of Paris, France, a young woman and a very fat man are seated at a side table. The room is about half full of customers talking in low murmurs. The lights are dim. Behind a large counter a man with a tired expression is operating a shining metal coffee machine. The young woman and the fat man have just finished eating dinner. A waitress arrives with a bottle and glass on a tray.

Sound: *Dishes clinking in the background.*

Marie: Your tonic water with lime, M'sieur Austin.

Sound: *A glass being set on the table.*

Howard: Thank you very much, Marie.

Sound: *Hissing of tonic water being poured into a glass.*

Howard *(to Rita)*: So, Miss Fowler . . . I suppose I don't quite fit your idea of an international spy, eh? You expected someone dashing, handsome, a man of the world . . . not, I'm afraid, someone like me.

Rita: Well, I must admit you were a bit of a . . .

Howard: Letdown?

Rita *(choosing the best word)*: A . . . surprise.

Howard *(laughs)*: You didn't expect an American agent in Paris to be overweight, middle-aged, dressed in a wrinkled business suit, and able to speak only passable French and German.

Rita *(laughing)*: Oh, Mr. Austin.

Howard: I understand how you feel. You are disappointed.

Rita: Not necessarily, Mr. Austin. I wanted to write about a *real* secret agent. Since my sources say you are one, then you're what I came for.

Howard: That's very kind of you. But still, you are a writer, young and full of romantic ideas. You must have hoped to fill your story with mysterious figures in the night, messages delivered by dark-cloaked foreigners, and chases through back alleys to elude capture.

Rita *(realizing she had)*: Perhaps.

Howard: Instead you are spending a dull evening in a dull restaurant with a dull American—why, you might as well have stayed home, eh?

Rita: If this is one of the places where you work, I want to write about it.

Howard: Excellent! Where shall we begin?

Sound: *Footsteps approaching.*

Marie: Pardon, M'sieur Austin.

Howard: Yes, Marie?

Marie: A telephone call, M'sieur Austin. I have brought the phone.

Sound: *Rattle of telephone being set down on table, then of receiver being picked up.*

Howard *(into the telephone)*: Yes? Yes. No. Thank you!

Sound: *Click of receiver being set down again.*

Howard *(to Rita)*: Well, take heart, my young friend. Perhaps your article will have a bit of intrigue in it yet.

Rita: How's that?

Howard: If you will accompany me to my office, at midnight we will be visited by a courier I have been expecting for some days now. He will have with him a paper . . . a significant paper, one for which several people have risked their lives. Its importance is staggering. In fact, some day soon this paper may well change the course of history. There is drama in that thought, yes?

Rita *(impressed)*: I'm interested!

Howard: Its delivery to me is the next-to-last step of its journey into official American hands. If you agree not to interfere in any way, you may watch this rather prosaic transfer of momentous information.

Rita *(agreeing)*: Of course!

Howard: Very well. Come, then.

Sound: *Chairs scraping the floor as the two rise to leave.*

Howard: It's already past eleven. My office is not far, but still we must hurry. It wouldn't do to miss our appointment.

Narrator: Howard and Rita leave the restaurant and walk quickly toward Howard's office, a few blocks away. At around eleven-thirty they trudge up six flights of stairs toward Howard's office.

Sound: *Stairs creaking under footsteps.*

Howard (*breathing hard from the climb*): I'll never fathom why I chose an office on the sixth floor.

Rita: It *is* quite a climb.

Howard: I'm afraid you will find my office is as uninteresting as I am, Miss Fowler. It will not provide you with a very glamorous setting for your story.

Rita: Yet if that paper is as important as you say . . .

Howard: It is, believe me. It is. (*pause*) Here's my office.

Sound: *Keys jingling, metal scraping against metal as key is turned in lock, and then door creaking open.*

Howard: After you, Miss Fowler.

Narrator: Rita walks into the room, only to stop with a surprised gasp.

Rita (*whispering*): Someone's here. I can see an outline against the window!

Howard: It can't be the courier already. Let me turn on the light.

Sound: *Light switch clicking, then Rita gasping again.*

Howard *(recognizing the figure):* Well, well . . . Max! You gave me a start. I thought you were still in Istanbul.

Max: Who's she?

Howard: Forgive me. The surprise of seeing you, Max, deprived me of my manners for a moment. Miss Fowler, this extremely tall and muscular fellow is Max Kovsky. Max is . . . shall we say . . . a member of the opposition. Max, this is Miss Rita Fowler, a journalist from my own country. She is here to write about the dramatic moments in my life . . . if I can remember any.

Rita *(softly):* Hello.

Max: *(answers with a grunt)*

Howard: Conversation isn't Max's strong point, Miss Fowler. I must say, his conscience is rather weak too. I have seen him persuade his enemies to do his bidding by the merest twist of their arms. In fact, the police of this and a number of other cities would like to talk to Max about certain unsolved cases . . . if they could only find him. Luckily, Max and I have never had to come to blows with each other. I hate to think what I might look like if we did.

Rita *(under her breath)*: Yes, he's quite a bruiser.

Howard *(peeved)*: I really must complain to the management. This is the second time in a month—the second time—that some scoundrel has gained access to my room from that confounded balcony!

Max: Balcony? I used a passkey I got from a custodian. I didn't know about the balcony. It might have saved me some trouble. The custodian wasn't exactly happy to give me the key.

Howard *(dryly)*: I'm sure. *(to Rita)* You see, Miss Fowler, before this building was converted to offices, this room used to be part of a large apartment. The room next door, formerly the living room, has the balcony, which happens to extend under *my* window as well. You can get onto it from the vacant room two doors down, which is just what somebody did last month. The management promised to block it off, but they haven't.

Max: Enough idle chatter! Where's the report?

Howard: Report? What report?

Max: Don't stall, Howard. The report on the new missile sites. I know you got it tonight.

Howard: As usual, your intelligence network is a trifle inadequate, Max. The report hasn't been delivered yet. It's due at midnight.

Max *(determined)*: Then I'll just wait for it.

Howard: Oh? You intend to intercept it?

Max *(menacingly)*: Maybe I won't have to. Maybe if I just twist this woman's arm a bit, you'll hand it over to me.

Rita *(frightened)*: You . . . you wouldn't! Mr. Austin!

Howard *(calmly)*: Now, now, Max. This young woman is in my company. Hurting her just to get at me would be very distressing behavior on your part.

Max *(sinisterly)*: Just hand the report over to me and there'll be no trouble. Otherwise I might have to twist *your* arm a little, Howard. You've bamboozled me out of too many deals over the years. A broken arm might make you think twice about trying to trick me in the future.

Howard: I should say it would—but why anticipate violence at this early stage? Why don't we just wait until the courier arrives and then discuss what to do?

Max: Okay, Howard, but no funny stuff. You know I'm hard to knock down and even harder to keep down. So we'll just sit quietly for the next quarter hour.

Howard *(correcting him)*: Sixteen minutes, Max. Sixteen minutes.

Sound: *Clock ticking.*

Narrator: The three sit noiselessly in the room, tensely waiting for the courier's knock at the door. Rita keeps her eyes on Max, who clenches and unclenches his fists the whole time. Howard sits calmly in a side chair. The powerful man's threats don't seem to worry him. As midnight approaches, Howard strikes up another conversation.

Howard: You know, Max, I really wish I knew how you learned about the paper.

Max: And we wish we knew how it got out of our country. Once we discovered it was gone, though, I just figured you'd come across it sooner or later. Anyway, not much harm has been done. In a few minutes I'll have it back, and . . .

Sound: *Loud rapping on the door.*

Max *(startled and anxious)*: What's that?

Howard *(calmly)*: The police, I should think. I thought that so momentous a package as we were expecting tonight might well deserve a little *extra* protection. Shall I let them in?

Max *(sharply)*: Stay away from that door!

Sound: *More loud rapping on the door.*

Howard: Very well, but if I don't answer, they will no doubt enter anyway. The door is unlocked, and I'm sure they won't hesitate to aim their service revolvers at someone who is so obviously an intruder. What will you do now, Max?

Sound: *Louder rapping on the door.*

Narrator: For a few moments Max is silent. His eyes dart around the room. Suddenly his gaze fixes on the window.

Max: The balcony! The balcony shall be a convenient exit for me. It was so kind of you to mention it. We shall meet again soon, very soon. Yes, Howard, I shall be waiting where you least expect to find me, and then we shall settle this little matter to my satisfaction!

Henri *(outside the door)*: M'sieur! M'sieur Austin!

Sound: *More loud rapping at the door, scraping of window sliding open, then distant sound of traffic roaring and honking.*

Max: Good-bye, Howard—for the moment. I'll be waiting for you—somewhere!

Sound: *Scraping sound and rattling of glass as Max climbs through the window, then footsteps moving toward the door, doorknob turning, creak of door opening.*

Howard: Come in, Henri.

Sound: *Footsteps entering the room.*

Henri: Ah, M'sieur Austin . . . so it *is* you. When nobody answered, I was afraid that perhaps some burglars—

Howard: No, Henri, nothing so dramatic, I'm afraid. Just old Howard Austin, working late as usual. It's very kind of you to look in, though.

Henri: Well, if I can be of any service to M'sieur—

Howard: I think not, Henri. We have all that we require.

Henri: In that case, M'sieur Austin, goodnight.

Sound: *Footsteps going out, door closing.*

Howard *(calmly)*: Would you care for a glass of tonic water, Miss Fowler, with a twist of lime? I always keep a bottle chilled in my office.

Rita *(confused, stammering)*: But . . . the police . . .

Howard: There were no police, my friend. There was just Henri, the night custodian, whom I was expecting. You see, Henri always makes his rounds at this hour, and if he sees light under my door, he invariably knocks . . . just to ascertain that all is as it should be.

Rita: But you told Max—

Howard *(suavely)*: A little ruse, my
young friend.

Rita: But . . . but Max may come back
off that balcony any second and
then—

Howard: I think not. In fact, I doubt
that Max will ever trouble me again.
You see, Miss Fowler, this office
really has no balcony.

Talk about it!

1 Rita thought Howard Austin was dull. How might the Midnight Visitor have changed her mind?

2 Why does the playwright keep telling us that Howard is dull?

3 Rita wants to write about a real secret agent. What important events might she include as she describes the evening with Howard Austin?

4 What makes this play enjoyable? Explain your answer.

5 In many suspense and mystery stories, seemingly unimportant information has become very important by the time the problem is solved. What information in this selection fits that description?

Bibliography

The Nicholas Factor by *Walter Dean Myers. Viking.* Gerald is asked by a government agent to spy on a group that is up to no good.

The Remarkable Return of Winston Potter Crisply by *Eve Rice. Greenwillow.* A humorous story about a brother and sister who set up a spying operation.

David Wolf — Secret Agent *(microcomputer program). Dynamix.* Play the role of a spy in this series of five adventures.

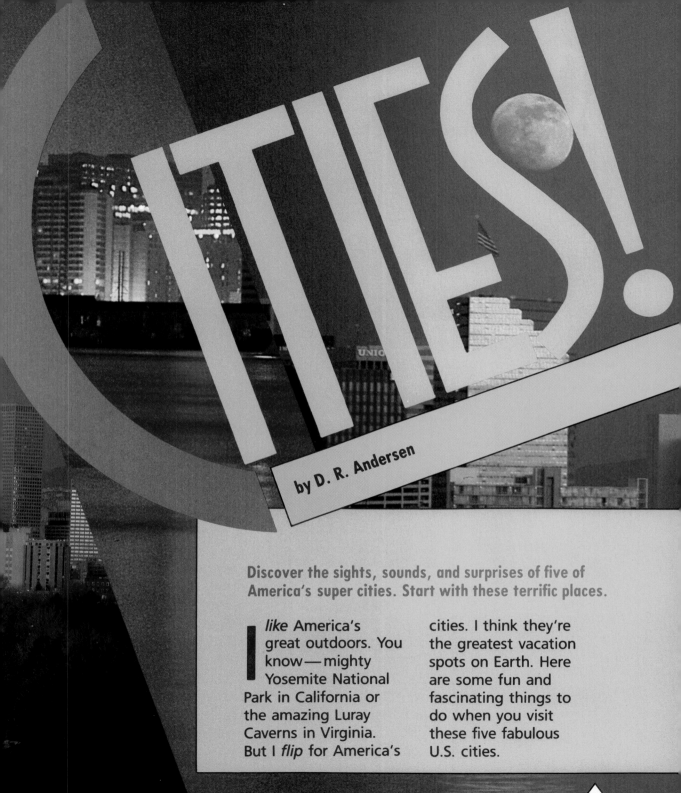

CITIES!

by D. R. Andersen

Discover the sights, sounds, and surprises of five of America's super cities. Start with these terrific places.

I *like* America's great outdoors. You know—mighty Yosemite National Park in California or the amazing Luray Caverns in Virginia. But I *flip* for America's cities. I think they're the greatest vacation spots on Earth. Here are some fun and fascinating things to do when you visit these five fabulous U.S. cities.

BOSTON

MASSACHUSETTS

Get acquainted with Boston by taking one of its many walking tours. The most intriguing tour, I believe, is the Black Heritage Trail. It includes many important sites in African-American history. Don't miss the Abiel Smith School on Smith Court. It was the first public school for African-American children. You'll also enjoy the African Meeting House on Smith Court. It is the oldest surviving church for African Americans. Take a walk among the old wooden buildings surrounding the

Would you like to step back into American history or explore the wonders of the sea? Then Boston might be just your cup of tea.

meeting house. Let your imagination take you back to life in the 1800's!

2 If you'd like some "fishy fun," make your next stop the New England Aquarium. You'll find it on Central Wharf on the waterfront. Step inside and you'll notice that the aquarium is dimly lit. This is to make you feel as if you're under

the sea. The best part of this special place is the four-story ocean tank. It holds 187,000 gallons of water—as well as many kinds of fish, sea turtles, and sharks. As you walk around the tank, you may think the sea

creatures are watching *you*. And they are! If you have time, hold a starfish, a crab, or a sea urchin in the Edge of the Sea Tidepool. Before you leave the wharf area, take in the dolphin and sea lion show nearby.

CHICAGO

ILLINOIS

Chicago is the *big* city. It has the world's *largest* inland port, the world's *tallest* building, and some *big* treats for travelers.

3 Extra! Extra! When you're in Chicago, read all about what's happening in these newspapers: the *Chicago Sun-Times* and the *Chicago Tribune.* Then tour the offices of each to find out how these big-city newspapers are written and printed. Attention, future reporters, editors, artists, printers, and cartoonists! This is an unbeatable opportunity to get an inside look at the world of newspapers.

Does the moon mystify you? Do you wonder about the stars? If so, you must visit the Adler Planetarium in Chicago. The changing sky shows will give you a unique view of the heavens. You'll also see exhibits on astronomy, telescopes, navigation, and space. Whether you're a rock hound or not, you'll get a thrill from the sight of the planetarium's moon rock!

4

DENVER
COLORADO

High up in the Rocky Mountains is a city out of the Wild West: Denver, Colorado. Nestled in the most beautiful mountains in the world, Denver is filled with sparkling reminders of its past.

5 Are you a coin collector? Maybe you just like to hear the jingle of coins in your pocket. No matter. You will be fascinated by the tour of the U.S. Mint in Denver. Here you'll get a glimpse of the whole coin-making process —from designing a coin to pressing the design onto the metal.

6 The cowhand and the Wild West are famous parts of our country's history. But did you know that many of America's cowhands were African Americans? Stop by Denver's Black American West Museum and learn about this forgotten history. You'll discover more than 5,000 items dating from 1859 to 1920. On display are boots, guns, saddles, buffalo hide coats, and much more. You can also enjoy the museum's taped interviews. These are lively accounts of the contributions that African Americans have made in the history of the West.

NEW ORLEANS

LOUISIANA

7 New Orleans has a rich ethnic history. It shows the influence of its Spanish and French settlers and of its African-American citizens. You'll find proof of these influences everywhere you look on a walking tour of the city's French Quarter. Lacy iron grillwork decorates the white and pastel Spanish-style houses. The smell of French doughnuts fills the air. The sound of a jazz trumpet echoes through the streets.

Some people call New Orleans America's most interesting city. Situated on the Mississippi River, New Orleans is like its famous fish and meat dish called jambalaya. It is a spicy, satisfying experience that you'll never forget.

Almost anywhere in New Orleans, listen and you'll hear a whistle in the distance. It's a steamboat—taking tourists on a trip up the Mississippi and back into New Orleans' past. Because of its river location, New Orleans has long been an important American port. You can feel the power of the Mississippi by taking the ferry that leaves from the foot of Canal Street. The Mississippi has magic and majesty such as no other river I know has.

SAN DIEGO

CALIFORNIA

San Diego is like a colorful painting. The sea and sky are blue. The tiled roofs are red. The trees and plants are green, with splashes of every other color of the rainbow. Here are two of what I consider to be San Diego's brightest spots.

9 Cabrillo National Monument is one of my favorite places on Earth. The view of San Diego and the bay is spectacular. You are sure to feel the

thrill that early Spanish and Portuguese explorers felt when they first discovered this wonderland over 400 years ago. History lovers will also enjoy stepping back in time in the old lighthouse museum. Nature lovers can observe sea life in tidepools and watch migrating whales (from December to mid-February). A visit to Cabrillo is the best

way to begin or end your tour of sensational San Diego.

10 Hup, two, three . . . march! Where? To the U. S. Naval Training Center. Watch the precision steps of the drill team, a group of sailors marching in military style. It's also exciting to take a tour of Navy frigates, cruisers, and destroyers at the end

of the Broadway pier. You'll get a real sense of what life aboard ship is like for the average sailor. You'll find yourself wondering whether you'd feel comfortable in one of those bunks on the high seas.

aybe now you can
see why I love Boston,
Chicago, Denver,
New Orleans, and San
Diego—and why I
urge you to visit them.
They offer inexpensive
and exciting treats
all year long.

Here's one last
travel tip: Don't limit
your explorations to
these five cities.
Whenever you're in a
new city, make the
most of it. Begin by
looking for a list of
special attractions.
Don't forget the zoo,
the parks, the
newspapers, the
museums, and musical
events. Remember—
it doesn't take a lot of
cash to cash in on city
fun. Before you know
it, you may find that
you, too, are a big fan
of America's super
cities!

1 Based on this article, which city would you most like to visit? Explain your answer.

2 What fun things to do or see in each city does the writer describe?

3 How does the writer try to convince you that American cities are the greatest vacation spots on Earth?

4 Imagine you are going to write an article about things to do or see in your own town or city. What things would you write about?

Bibliography

City/Country: A Car Trip in Photographs *by Ken Robbins. Viking Kestrel.* Beautiful photographs take you across America, contrasting city and country life.

Landmarks of Liberty. *Hammond.* This guide helps you explore 22 of America's most famous historical sites.

Where in the U.S.A. Is Carmen Sandiego? *(microcomputer program). Broderbrund.* Learn geography as you chase a master criminal across the country.

THE SUN CALLERS

from
PEOPLE OF THE SHORT BLUE CORN
by Harold Courlander

Throughout history people have tried to explain the world around them. See what you think of this Hopi Indian explanation for why the sun rises.

At a certain place north of Oraibi,[1] Coyote was living there, and a little beyond that the rooster was living. Now, it was in the dark of the night, and Coyote was going around looking for something to eat. There in the darkness he met the rooster, who was sitting on a high rock. He greeted the rooster, saying, "Ha'u," and the rooster greeted Coyote the same way.

Coyote said, "What are you doing there? Why are you not at home this time of the night?"

The rooster said, "I have work to do. I have to make the sun rise."

Coyote said, "You take yourself too seriously. Anyone can make the sun rise."

The rooster answered, "No, indeed, it is only I who can do it."

Coyote said, "On the contrary, I am the one who has the power to make the sun come up."

"Let us have a test," the rooster said. "Whoever makes the sun appear, he shall be acknowledged as the Sun Caller."

"That is good," Coyote said. "I will try first."

He sat back on his haunches, pointed his nose toward the sky, and howled to summon the sun. He went on doing this until he was breathless, but the sky remained as black as ever.

---

[1]Oraibi [ō•rī′ bē]

"Enough," the rooster said. "Now I will try." He stretched his neck, flapped his wings, and crowed. Once, twice, several times he crowed, but still the night was black.

Coyote said, "Now it is my turn," and again he howled until he was breathless, but around them there was still nothing but darkness.

The rooster said, "You are wasting your time. I will show you how it is done." He stretched his neck, flapped his wings, and crowed. Again and again he called the sun, but nothing happened.

"Now pay attention," Coyote said. "This is the way to do it." He put his nose up and howled with great feeling, telling the sun it was time to appear. But everything was still the same, and there was only darkness all around them.

They went on this way, taking turns all through the night. And one time after the rooster crowed, things were a little lighter. "You see," the rooster said, "I am beginning to do it."

Then Coyote tried again, and things were a little lighter still. Coyote said, "It is quite clear that I did better than you."

But the sun had not appeared, and the rooster tried once more. He filled his lungs with air, stretched his neck, flapped his wings, and crowed mightily.

And as he did so, the red edge of the sun appeared over the horizon.

"My friend," the rooster said, "you can judge for yourself. As anyone can see, it was I who brought the sun up from down below."

Coyote said, "Yes, I acknowledge it. You have powerful medicine. You are the Sun Caller."

Coyote went away. But he kept thinking, "I almost did it. Once when I called, the night grew a little lighter. Perhaps with practice I can do it." And even to this time, every so often in the night you can hear Coyote trying again to make the sun rise. But the rooster, he is the one that really does it. And because his work goes on and on without ever ending, he has grown hoarse. You can hear it for yourself.

Unit

3

Wondering about the moon leads a poet to write about a magical flight of fancy.

Some wacky sports fans are as fun to watch as the teams for which they cheer.

No one had ever crossed the Atlantic by balloon. Ben and Max were determined to be the first.

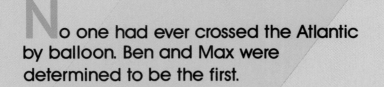

Find out how a group of Georgia students showed their town that kids can make a difference.

Downtown study set for Royston

By LINTON JOHNSON

Royston officials are promoting in its downtown area.

The NEWS L

Weekly Newsp

Franklin County's Award

Market st to area s

The Royston Involvement Project of Pupils for Lifting Economy and Society (RIPPLES) group has issued a shopper's survey in the Royston area to acquire input which will be used to help map a plan for the revitalization of the city's downtown.

Chris is nearly blind, yet she dreams of running on the middle-school track team.

117

The Kids Who Saved A Dying Town

by Bruce B. Henderson

A group of students were upset at how badly kept their downtown area looked. They wondered why someone didn't do something about it. Their teacher challenged them to be the ones to take some action! Could kids really make a difference?

On a Wednesday afternoon in September 1984, five gifted sixth-graders and their teacher walked through downtown Royston, Georgia. "Look at those ugly old buildings!" Julinna Oxley exclaimed, pointing to two adjoining boarded-up structures that appeared as if they might topple in a strong wind.

"Why doesn't someone do something about them?" asked Matt Wilson.

Julinna was writing down what the students saw on their "awareness walk." She noted the addresses of the offending buildings, located only a few doors from the intersection of Royston's main streets. During the next hour, Julinna's list grew, and the students became angered by what they observed. Six of the 36 buildings in the prime downtown area were vacant. There was litter everywhere, overgrown weeds, and peeling paint.

Then the students came to another eyesore: a pile of junked cars and trucks next to a city park.

"Why does the city allow it?" Judi Gurley wondered.

Alice Terry, their energetic teacher, had an idea: why not assign the class to find the answers?

Awareness Walk

JULINNA took pictures

119

Royston, population 2,650, is located 100 miles northeast of Atlanta and was founded in 1879. Once a thriving cotton center, it was now a town that time had passed by. Royston's one claim to fame was that baseball immortal Ty Cobb called it home. Now many natives had to move elsewhere to find work. Residents drove to neighboring towns to shop.

To Alice Terry's students, it was obvious that downtown Royston was dying. And no one was doing anything to stop the slide. When they returned to their classroom at Royston Elementary School, the students were unusually quiet. One of them said later, "I felt so sorry for Royston, I wanted to cry."

Alice Terry, who was married to the school's principal, had taught this group of gifted students for several years. Twice a week, on Wednesday and Friday afternoons, her job was to find special ways to inspire these young people, who needed stimulation beyond their regular schoolwork. She called this her "Challenge Class."

Now, sliding a chair over to the low table where the students were sitting, she asked a question. "Okay, we've identified some of our town's problems. What can we do to save Royston?" Action, not talk, was what she graded the students on.

"Someone has to tow the junked cars away," said Judi Gurley.

"Maybe we can get the owner of those two boarded-up buildings to fix them," added another student.

Alice scribbled furiously to keep up with the ideas that sprang forth. These students were bright and talented. Brandee Braswell was adept at dealing with people. Derrick Gable excelled in organization. Judi Gurley often played devil's advocate, taking an opposing view for the sake of discussion. Julinna Oxley had a talent for transforming ideas into sensible action. Matt Wilson was the artist of the group.

Calling their group RIPPLES—because they wanted to start a ripple effect among townspeople to revitalize Royston—the students decided to write public officials who could help. When RIPPLES learned that the owner of the two dilapidated buildings had refused either to sell or to renovate, they sent him a sharply worded letter. "The buildings are a fire hazard," they wrote. "Before we contact the state fire marshal, we strongly urge you to fix them up or sell them to someone who will."

One of the students suggested they also write to the owner of the auto-wrecking business about the rusting cars and trucks.

This is a news clipping about Project Ripples makes waves in Royston

AN OPEN LETTER TO THE CITIZENS OF

350 College Street
Royston GA 30662

ROYSTON
Royston Elementary

DEAR EDITOR,

We are involved in the RIPPLES project; ROYSTON INVOLVEMENT PROJECT for PUPILS for LIFTING the ECONOMY and SOCIETY.

In doing our downtown project we have identified many problems with the downtown area. One of the worst is the two wooden structures located next to Cunningham's Furniture Store in the center of town. We are working on some solutions to this problem. Th...

During ...
buildings nee...
significance ...
probably the ...
buildings are ...
They are as we...
were to burn,
also.

Since Royst...
National Histor...
more perfect r...
make Royston "...
these two buildi...
possible, not on...
downtown area ...
If the owne...
to restore them,...
responsible enoug...
talked to a p...
...restor...

Project Ripples makes waves in Royston

To The Editor:

We are involved in the RIPPLES project: ROYSTON INVOLVEMENT PROJECT for PUPILS for LIFTING the ECONOMY and SOCIETY.

In doing our downtown project we have identified many problems with the downtown area. One of the worst is the two wooden structures located next to Cunningham's Furniture Store in the center of town. We are working on some ... to this problem.

... probably burn also.

Since Royston is only one step short of becoming on the National Historic Register, we the kids in order to form a more perfect revitalization of Royston are going to try to make Royston "the pride of the foothills". We feel that these two buildings should be revitalized as soon as possible, not only to preserve them, but also to protect the downtown area.

We urge Mr. Howard Strickland and Mr. Jack Ridgway, the owners of these buildings, to join us and other interested citizens of Royston in making Royston a better place to live. We encourage them to either restore them for their own use or to sell these buildings if they have no interest in using them for a business.

We hope the citizens of Royston will join us in making PROJECT RIP-

PLES a project for all citizens of Royston and not just us kids.

Sincerely yours,
Derrick Gable
Matt Wilson
Judi Gurley
Julinna Ozley
Brandee Braswell
6th Grad...

Challenge students ... ing for a revita... community. Royst... mentary School.

... Jack Ridgway, ...d other ...ston a better ...restore them ...if they have

Royston vows to crack down on junk cars

by LINTON JOHNSON

The Royston City Council ...day night promised to ...tough on the junk car ...ation in town, vowing ...more strictly enforce ...ing city ordinances ...ricting junk cars.

..."it's not a business," ...Councilman Jeff Fra-

"I want the ordi-...ces enforced."

...e other council mem-...agreed, and the en-...ement is to begin ...ediately. All junk cars ...o be removed from the ...limits, or their owners ...Neal urged Wallace and ...Charles Payne t-

can expect to wind up in city court.

Dealers in the junk business are required to erect fences or shrubbery to hide their junk cars, according to City Attorney Jerry Neal.

In other business, the council decided to allow van conversion to be conducted in a building owned by G.L. Wallace of 549 Church St. Previously, the building has been used for the changing to automobiles into convertibles.

"common sense" in the process of their work, respecting the rights of their neighbors. Payne said that only four or five vans per week would be customized at the site, and the noisier aspects of the process will be conducted during daytime hours.

Following up on a Jan. 14 council discussion, Neal said that Howard Strickland plans to either rent... sell his part of ...Street ...

way, who owns the other part of the building, also plans to sell his share of the downtown structure.

Councilman Jerry Gaines reported that city mechanic Mark Hartley said that 90 percent of the trouble with the city vehicles is due to abuse on the part of city employees. The council agr— 1 to keep a closer ...the use of city ...

Member Sally ...stion that the ...commendat— ...s of several ...for their ...

extra efforts during the recent hard freeze was approved. Gas employees Edwin James and Billy Conley, Billy Bryson, Marty Echols and Paul Brown of the water department and Jerry Bowen of the street department were praised for their work during that time.

After several minutes of executive session requested by Neal, the council discussed two possibilities concerning the city's wine ordinance. One would prohibit the sale of wine in the city altogether, while the

other would restrict the current ordinance so that wine could not be sold within a certain distance of schools and churches.

"I'd like to get some feedback on this one," said Councilman Wayne Braswell. Beard also warned against making "a hasty decision," and the matter was tabled until the next meeting.

Frazier reported his findings concerning the council's policy on stray dogs. He checked with Royston Animal Hospital's Dr. Doris Cato, who said her

facility would keep a maximum of five dogs up to five days for $4 per day for small dogs and $5 per day for large dogs. If the dogs are not picked up within five days, they would be destroyed at $10 each.

The council asked Councilman Ray Phillips to check with the dogcatcher in Elberton before making a decision on the matter.

Mrs. Lane brought up what she called a litter problem in Royston and noted that "we have to reach the people to make them proud of their city

again. We have to ... the attitude."

She said this goe with the downtown ization program, council will discuss ideas concering the ion.

The council also ap payment of a te $1,728 to the C Municipal Associati construction of it building in Atlant city's share will be out over two equal payments of $864 M 1985, and March 1.

The class soon learned that the junked vehicles were on land belonging to the railroad. They decided to alert railroad officials. Alice Terry wrote, "I am a teacher of gifted students who are doing a year-long project on the revitalization of our downtown area. Your property, leased by King's Auto to park wrecked cars and trucks, is an eyesore. We ask that you take immediate action."

Things were beginning to stir in Royston. But a few merchants were upset because the students were bringing civic problems to the public's attention. This seemed "too negative" to them.

In January the students received a late Christmas present. Alice told them, "I have good news. Those two old buildings went up for sale yesterday!"

The students were stunned momentarily. Then they shouted, "We did it! They listened to us!"

"Congratulations!" Alice called out over the clamor. "All right," she said. "What should we do next?"

"Let's ask the town to buy the buildings and restore them," one student suggested.

The following week RIPPLES asked the city council to pay for a survey of residents and merchants. They hoped this would identify the causes of Royston's problems. After two weeks of study, Mayor John Beard called Alice. "Tell your students we'll do the survey."

One questionnaire asked residents, "How often do you shop in downtown Royston?" "What kinds of businesses do you patronize?" "If new retail establishments were developed, what types of stores and services would you use?"

The merchants were asked, "How would you rate the downtown area for quality of eating places, parking, and cleanliness of streets?" "What do you think is the primary reason why people don't shop in Royston?"

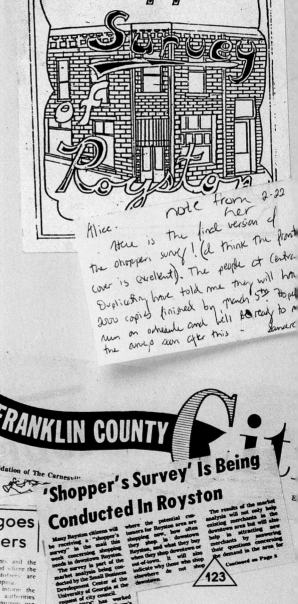

note from 2-22

Alice,
Here is the final version of the shoppers survey! (I think the front cover is excellent). The people at Central Duplicating have told me they will have 2000 copies finished by march 5th. Hopefully run on schedule and will be ready to mail the surveys soon after this. — Sandra

Downtown study set for Royston

By LINTON JOHNSON

promoting in its downtown area."

Royston officials are hoping to...

The NEWS L

Franklin County's Award

...study for Royston...
Mrs. Terry said...
well-received.

...has been involved in the downtown revitalization project and will help form topics and questions for the study. Their teacher, Alice Terry, is a member of Royston's Downtown Development Authority.

"We hope to find out if people are shopping in Royston and why, if they are not shopping in Royston and why," Mrs. Terry said. "What do you...

...survey would be distributed in the next few weeks with results expected within two months.
The study will point information in several areas:
— Trade Area: Bound: Detailed description of geographic area which downtown most of its retail customers. This includes...

Wookly Newspaper

Market study goes to area shoppers

The Royston Involvement Project of Pupils for Lifting Economy and Society (RIPPLES) group has issued a shopper's survey in the Royston area to acquire input which will be used to help map a path for the revitalization of the city's downtown business...

...help merchants and the city understand where the potential customers are presently shopping.
It will also inform the revitalization authorities how often consumers use the downtown shops and stores.

FRANKLIN COUNTY

A Consolidation of The Carnesville...

'Shopper's Survey' Is Being Conducted In Royston

Many Royston citizens will be receiving a "shopper's survey" in the mail this week concerning shopping needs in downtown Royston.
The survey is part of the market analysis being conducted by the Small Business Development Center of the University of Georgia at the request of city council.
The SBDC has worked closely with Alice Terry's Challenge Class Elementary...

...where the potential customers for Royston area are, how often shopping now, what they buy, when they shop downtown or out-of-town. It will also indicate why those who shop elsewhere do not shop downtown.

The results of the market analysis will not only help existing merchants in the downtown area but will also help in attracting new merchants by answering their questions concerning the demand in the area for...

Continued on Page 3

The results showed that the residents were discouraged from shopping in Royston because of limited merchandise, poor store appearance, and a lack of competitive prices. Nearly all residents said they would shop in Royston if the downtown area were improved. The members of RIPPLES were now sure that the townspeople were with them.

In early February, Alice found a letter from the railroad in her mailbox. That afternoon, she opened it in front of her class. Inside was a copy of the railroad's certified letter to King's Auto, demanding that the junked cars be moved from railroad property immediately. The students cheered when Alice finished. Within a few weeks, there wasn't a junked vehicle in sight.

Meanwhile the group found a turn-of-the-century picture that showed the two dilapidated buildings, which were then well maintained and sturdy. Matt, the artist, went to work on a drawing to show how the structures might look restored.

We found this picture of the wood building it was enough for us to know what it looked like.

ROYSTON COCA-COLA BOTTLING COMPANY--Mr. A.F. Bell, Sr., his son, Flynn Bell, Jr., and two workers for the Royston Coca-Cola Bottling Co. stand in front of the Royston Coca-Cola Bottling Co. The 1913 Model T. Ford truck the 1913 Model T International truck were used to transport bottles of Coke. The worker on the far left is Mr. Seaborn J. Jordan of Royston and the worker on the right is Mr. Pickeny Randall of Royston. The young boy in the picture, Mr. Flynn Bell, Jr., is the current president of the Hartwell Coca-Cola Bottling Company.

Next the students fashioned a proposal for the city to buy the buildings, and then they went to the city council. "You can buy both buildings for a few thousand dollars," Alice told council members. "There would be an additional expense in restoring them. But the Chamber of Commerce needs an office, and you can rent the other one to bring in revenue."

Two weeks later, Brandee, whose father was on the city council, came to class with news that the council had voted to buy the two buildings. The students jumped out of their chairs and hugged each other.

"It's as if we're adults instead of kids," one student said. "People are listening to our ideas."

But then came bad news. "The buildings were sold to someone else," Mayor Beard reported to Alice Terry one day. "We didn't move quickly enough. A person named Gerald Carey bought them."

"That's not fair!" Matt shouted when he heard the news.

"It's not the end of the world," Alice said quietly. "What did you set out to accomplish?"

"To restore the buildings," Julinna answered.

"Right," Alice said. "Maybe you can still accomplish that."

"Let's go talk to the new owner. Maybe we can get *him* to restore the buildings," Brandee suggested.

Matt's 1st picture of improving them.

During a phone conversation with Alice Terry, Gerald Carey made his position clear. "No bunch of kids is going to tell me what to do with my property," he warned. But he grudgingly agreed to talk with them.

At the meeting, the students began telling him what they had in mind. Carey, a native of Royston, was impressed by Matt's sketches. Half an hour later, he was smiling and agreeing how nice the buildings would look restored. "May I keep these drawings to show my contractor so he'll know what I want done?" he finally asked.

125

On the afternoon of May 15, 1985, "Detour—Road Closed" signs went up on Royston's main streets. Traffic was diverted as a horde of young students descended on the downtown area. Their mission: to clean up the city's cluttered streets.

When the idea of a student work detail was first discussed, one of Alice's fellow teachers scoffed, "No kid is going to volunteer for cleanup work." But the RIPPLES members talked up the project and presented a skit to fourth-, fifth-, and sixth-graders, acting out highlights in the history of Royston. On cleanup day, 140 students appeared. They swept sidewalks, cleared alleys, and washed storefronts. They pulled weeds and planted flowers.

'Renewal Day' set for improvement projects

By LINTON JOHNSON

Plans have been finalized for the "Renewal Day" for downtown Royston's revitalization Wednesday, May 15.

Alice Terry, the Downtown Task Force member who is organizing the day's activities, said the state Department of Transportation has approved blocking off Ga. 17 (Church Street) between the hours of 1 p.m. for the

children (pending Board of Education approval), city employees, city police, Franklinia Garden Club members, downtown merchants and anyone else who'd like to help.

The primary focus will be on the city park at the railroad tracks, where a plan for the park drawn by the University of Georgia will begin to be implemented, with the supervision of members of the garden club and city personnel.

Merchants have been asked to put in requests

Royston - Franklin Springs Chamber of Commerce, are co-sponsoring a poster and essay contest for grades K-3 and 4-6 on the theme "My Town."

Also, members of the student group Project RIPPLES were to share a program on Royston's history with their fellow fourth - through -sixth graders earlier this week, and the students will see a film on the Main Street program Friday, May 10.

The 35-minute film, with a focus on downtown revitalization, will also be shown to the general

Teachers rolled up their sleeves, too. So did merchants, store employees, and even onlookers who found themselves drawn into a community effort the likes of which Royston had never seen before.

In the middle of all this activity were the two old buildings. Gerald Carey had given the kids permission to start ripping down loose shingles. Inside one building, Carey himself was at work with a crew.

"Hello, Mr. Carey," the RIPPLES students hollered, happy to see "their" buildings being renovated. The student with the biggest grin was Matt Wilson, who could recognize his drawings coming to life.

On May 22, 1985, the last day of school, the sixth-graders and their teacher sat around the same table where they had first discussed the plan to revitalize their town. By now a discount drugstore chain had looked at the city council's survey and decided to open a store in Royston. A supermarket chain was also coming.

"What have you learned from all this?" Alice Terry asked.

"That you have to care enough to do something," replied Julinna.

Today the two restored buildings are the home of a new clothing store. Though still not a boomtown, Royston has begun to come back to life. City planners have written an optimistic master plan for further development. Royston has become a town with a future.

Chamber of Commerce president Greg Hall said, "Before RIPPLES we had little growth in five years. Now we have over twenty new businesses. Our town has more potential than ever."

On September 26, 1986, Alice Terry and her students walked onto the stage of a large auditorium in Washington, D.C., before 300 spectators. Donald P. Hodel, Secretary of the Interior, read a proclamation: "This group of perceptive, energetic young people proved the educational system can make a dynamic contribution to the preservation movement and inspire the teamwork necessary to promote change. For their creativity, ingenuity, and perseverance, Brandee Braswell, Derrick Gable, Judi Gurley, Julinna Oxley, and Matt Wilson of RIPPLES, and their inspiring instructor, Alice Terry, are granted the Public Service Award of the Department of the Interior."

When the applause and standing ovation came, so did Alice Terry's tears. Surrounded by her students, she knew that everyone can make a difference. Kids too. We only have to try.

"The real RIPPLES GANG!!"

Talk about it!

1 How did the students make a difference?

2 Do you believe that all of us, including kids, can make a difference if we try? Explain your answer.

3 Describe the important events that happened in each of the following months during the RIPPLES project: September 1984, January 1985, February 1985, May 1985, September 1986.

4 Would you enjoy being invovled in a project like RIPPLES? Explain your answer.

5 At what point in the selection did you first think that the students' actions were beginning to make a difference? Explain your answer.

Bibliography

Cities 2000 by Christopher Pick. Facts on File. Looks at the past and future of urban development.

New Providence: A Changing City Scape by Renata Tscharner. Harcourt Brace Jovanovich. A made-up city is examined at six points during the twentieth century.

Smalltown U.S.A. (film). NBC. Examines how change has affected three small towns in different parts of the country.

WACKY SPORTS FANS

BY MIR TAMIM ANSARY

When you talk about the legendary figures of sports, don't forget some of the outstanding fans— especially the wacky ones.

Many people enjoy football and baseball, and are dedicated fans of their favorite teams. In fact, some fans are so dedicated, they're downright wacky. Which sport has the wackiest fans—football or baseball? Read on and make your own decision.

Lou SanGiovanni

grew up in New York City, where he was a devoted fan of the New York Giants football team. He still loves the Giants, but he now resides in California. He can't watch his favorite team in person. He can't even watch them on television, for most Giants' games are televised only in the New York City area. That's why every Sunday when the Giants are playing, Lou calls his mother, who lives near New York City. She puts the phone next to the television, turns up the volume, and retires to another room. Lou spends the next three hours listening to the game. He may be the only sports fan in the world who follows football by telephone.

Few fans have achieved the status of a legend. Hilda Chester was among the few. Everyone who saw the Brooklyn Dodgers play baseball knew who she was. Hilda, who rarely missed a game, applauded by banging frying pans together, ringing brass bells, and clanging a cowbell. She made the most commotion, however, with her loud voice. All of Brooklyn came to know her as "the First Lady."

One day Hilda went to watch her beloved Brooklyn Dodgers play in Philadelphia. Philadelphia also had a famous loud-voiced fan, "Leather Lung" Pete Adelis. Pete bought the seat right next to Hilda's. Few of the spectators in the park that day recall much about the game. The real duel was in the stands—a shouting match between the First Lady and Leather Lung Pete. Who won? Philadelphia fans say Leather Lung Pete triumphed. Brooklyn fans claim the victor was the First Lady.

UNIVERSITY OF NEBRASKA

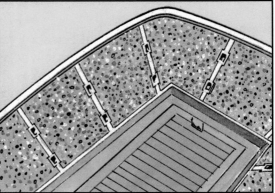

UNIVERSITY OF HAWAII VS NEBRASKA — TODAY

The University of Nebraska football team must have some of the world's most loyal fans. On December 6, 1976, sixteen thousand of them saw their squad play the football team from the University of Hawaii. This wouldn't have been peculiar, but the game was played in Honolulu. Sixteen thousand Nebraskans had flown to Hawaii merely to watch a football game.

Few individuals can rival baseball fan Diana Deis for loyalty. One year when Diana's favorite team, the Milwaukee Brewers, was performing poorly, Diana climbed to the top of a 40-foot tower. She announced that she would be there every day until the Brewers won seven games in a row. For the next two months, Diana spent 18 hours a day in the tower, coming down only to sleep. Alas, the Brewers didn't win seven games in a row. Finally Diana got pneumonia and had to abandon her lonely post.

Valdis Slakans of Galveston, Texas, calls himself the world's greatest Detroit Lions fan. Valdis has never been to Detroit and has never seen the Lions play football. Yet every Sunday he dons his Lions jacket and goes to his local stadium. There he unfurls a banner that reads, "V. J. Slakans, World's Greatest Dee-troit Lions Fan." Valdis pays absolutely no attention to the teams on the field. He tunes his shortwave radio to a Detroit station and listens to the game the Lions are playing, sometimes over a thousand miles away.

When Larry Loebers heard that the Cincinnati baseball stadium was being torn down, he stopped by to see if he could buy some souvenirs. Once there, Larry was overcome with nostalgia, remembering all the happy moments he had spent at the stadium. As Larry explains, "One thing just led to another." By the time he left, Larry had bought both dugouts, the clubhouse furnishings, the bullpens, the foul poles, the scoreboard, part of the outfield wall, a popcorn stand, a ticket booth, and four hundred seats.

For Larry Stakenas, the most thrilling aspect of a ball game is the chance to take home a ball. Such opportunities come frequently in baseball games. Once, however, Larry came within inches of catching the ball at a football game. He was sitting in the bleachers behind the end zone, just above the band, when a field goal was kicked. As soon as the ball went up, Larry had an intuition that it would land near his seat. His pulse racing, he watched the ball arc over the goalposts. He got ready. As the ball came down, he leaped out of his seat, jumped over the wall—and landed right inside a tuba.

Talk about it!

1 In what ways are the fans described in the selection wacky?

2 Juding from the fans described in this selection, which sport—baseball or football—do you think has the wackiest fans? Explain your answer.

3 What is your opinion of these wacky fans? Would you like to meet any of them? Explain your answer.

Bibliography

Encyclopedia Brown's Book of Wacky Sports *by Donald Sobol. Morrow.* A collection of zany and wacky events in football, baseball, boxing, and other sports.

Giant Book of More Strange but True Sports Stories *by Howard Liss. Random House.* Unusual but true incidents from the world of sports.

Big Moments in Sports *(film). Sterling.* Highlights from basketball, football, baseball, and other sports.

The Flight of the Double Eagle

by Peter Jaret

Ben and Max both had a dream—
to cross the Atlantic Ocean in a balloon.
Could they succeed when so many
others had tried and failed?

1 Ben Abruzzo gasped and shivered. Wind
was driving icy rain into the boat-shaped
gondola hanging from the balloon *Double
Eagle*. Ben and his best friend, Max Anderson,
were riding in that small gondola above the
storm-lashed waters of the Atlantic Ocean. Two
days before, they had set out to do what no one
had ever done before—cross the Atlantic Ocean
in a balloon. Sixteen times in the past, balloonists
had attempted the flight, but no one had
succeeded—and five balloonists had died trying.

139

The storm was the worst one Ben had ever seen. He looked at Max with envy. Max, who was wearing layers of wool clothing covered by a rain poncho, was sleeping peacefully. Ben, however, was soaked to the skin, and he shook uncontrollably. The rain, freezing as it fell, coated Ben's face and clothes with a layer of ice. Every time Ben moved, the ice cracked and shattered like glass. He had never been so cold in his life.

Looking over the edge of the gondola to the ocean 400 feet below, Ben saw waves breaking over giant chunks of floating ice. The storm had blown the balloon off course, hurling it north toward Greenland instead of east toward Europe. Ice forming on the balloon kept dragging it down toward the ocean. Ben took the balloon up to 5,300 feet, listening to the high-pitched whine of the distress beacon he had turned on a short time before. He knew that he was in danger of freezing. He knew that if help did not come quickly, he and Max would die.

Six hours later Ben and Max were taken aboard a Navy helicopter in a daring rescue from the storm-tossed seas. They had flown the balloon for more than 65 hours, flown it in worse weather than any other balloonists had ever encountered. They had landed the balloon in the ocean under nearly impossible conditions—and survived.

Others may have been impressed, but not Ben and Max. They had failed to cross the Atlantic. Nothing else seemed to count for them. When Ben faced the reporters at the airfield in Iceland, he looked exhausted and terribly disappointed. During the bitter cold of the flight, his left foot had become frostbitten. The pain was so bad that he could hardly walk. "It was an interesting trip," Ben told the crowd of reporters, "but one that I will never make again."

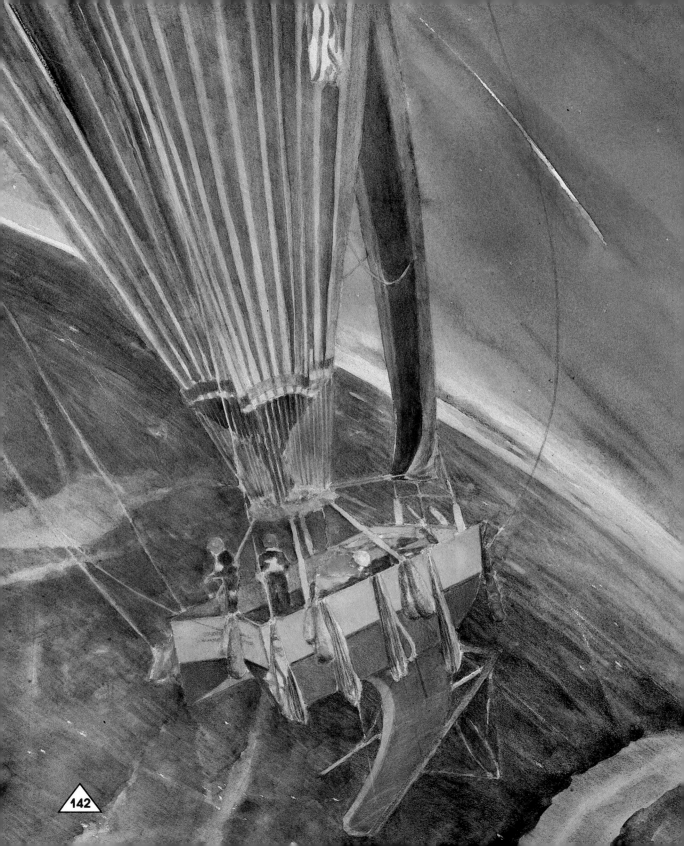

One year later another balloon, called the *Double Eagle II,* loomed over a field in Presque Isle, Maine. Three men stood in the open gondola, ready to fly across the Atlantic Ocean. They were Ben Abruzzo, Max Anderson, and Larry Newman.

Max had never given up the idea of a transatlantic balloon flight. Scarcely two days after his and Ben's rescue at sea, Max began thinking about another attempt. However, he had trouble convincing Ben to think about it. Ben's foot was still hurting badly, and he was still suffering from the disappointment of the first attempt. "Max, why should we do this?" he wanted to know.

"It's a way of entering history," Max said. "We'd be doing something that has fired people's imaginations, something that has always seemed impossible. I think I can do it, Ben, and I think you can too."

Ben responded grumpily at first, but gradually his sense of adventure returned. Finally he consented to join Max in the daring venture.

The two balloonists decided that they needed a third pilot. They chose Larry Newman, a young friend of Ben's. Larry was an expert with radios, and he had certain other skills that neither Ben nor Max possessed.

The three men planned the flight of the *Double Eagle II* with great care. The new balloon was bigger than *Double Eagle I* because it had to carry the weight of one more man. The balloonists packed seafarers' clothing—wool and waterproof garments that would keep them warm and dry. With the help of their ground crew, they designed a new, more effective rain cover for the gondola.

By August the balloon was ready, and so were the supplies. Even the weather was perfect. A storm was heading toward Maine from the west. The balloonists had worked out a plan to ride the front edge of this storm the way a surfer rides the edge of a wave. In a few hours the storm would move out across the Atlantic Ocean toward Europe. If the balloonists could maintain sufficient altitude, they would ride just ahead of the bad weather. With the force of the storm propelling them, they hoped to ride all the way to Europe.

At 8:42 P.M. on August 11, 1978, *the Double Eagle II* began its flight. As the balloon rose into the dark night, Max felt a great sense of peace. He knew that he and his partners had done all they could to prepare for the flight. He knew he could accept whatever happened now, whether it was a success or a failure. Ben, too, felt calm and confident.

Larry, however, could hardly contain his excitement as he looked out from the small gondola. The balloon was part of the wind, moving so silently that Larry could hear dogs barking and people talking thousands of feet below. Stars glittering in the night sky and meteors streaking across the darkness created a scene of breathtaking beauty.

The flight began well. On the morning of the second day, after 38 hours in the air, the *Double Eagle II* passed over the coast of Newfoundland and headed out over the Atlantic Ocean. Each day, in the heat of the sun, the helium gas inside the balloon expanded, and the balloon rose. When the helium expanded, some of it escaped through a vent in the side of the balloon. Then in the late afternoon, when the remaining helium cooled, the balloon began to fall. To keep the balloon from descending too far, the balloonists threw overboard bags of sand, or ballast.

Ballast is extra weight carried in a balloon specifically to be thrown away. The more helium a balloon loses, the less weight it can hold aloft. Balloonists throw away ballast to make the balloon lighter. Once the ballast has been used up, the balloon's own weight drags it down after a while.

Ben kept careful track of how much ballast had been used. By the second day he could see that the ballast would run out in four more days. He began to worry. Was the balloon moving fast enough to reach Europe in four days? If not, the balloon would drop down somewhere in the Atlantic Ocean.

He had another agonizing concern as well—the cold. His frostbitten foot had never fully recovered. He knew that if his foot froze again, it might never heal. For that reason, he had brought along battery-heated socks. He had to keep changing the batteries and inspecting the socks to make sure they were working.

On the third night the *Double Eagle II* floated 14,000 feet above the Atlantic Ocean. Ben noticed that the balloon was slowly descending. Ice had formed on the balloon, weighing it down.

Ben tried to puncture a sandbag but his knife glanced off the bag. The sand, packed wet, had frozen! Ben found a hammer and began pounding the bag, desperately trying to release enough sand to keep the balloon from descending any farther. Chunks of frozen sand fell away, but the balloon continued to fall. For six hours they struggled. Finally Larry managed to hold the balloon steady at 13,500 feet

After that icy night, the three men were relieved to see a bright sun at dawn. The fourth day of the flight promised to be a balmy one. When Max looked back toward North America, however, he could see that the storm following them was getting closer. If the balloon climbed above 18,000 feet, they would stay ahead of the storm. Below 18,000 feet, however, they would be swept into a caldron of whirlwinds, rain, and snow.

Tense and uneasy, the balloonists waited for the morning sun to warm the helium. When the balloon reached 20,000 feet, they relaxed. Now all they had to do was keep the balloon at that altitude.

That evening, as Ben, Max, and Larry dropped off ballast, Ben calculated that the ballast would run out in two more nights. Max believed that they could reach Europe by then—if only they could keep the balloon high enough.

On the morning of the fifth day, disaster struck. Max was heating soup in a pan, Ben was gathering ballast for that evening, and Larry was watching the instruments. Suddenly, mysteriously, the balloon began to descend.

"We're going down!" Larry shouted, watching the meter that showed the balloon's altitude.

"How fast?" Ben asked.

"Four hundred feet a minute," Larry said, reading the meter. Ben threw a small amount of ballast overboard, but the *Double Eagle II* continued to descend.

"What's happening?" Max wondered, his voice cracking with tension.

Ben was busy calculating with a pencil and paper. Finally he declared, "If we use up any more ballast, we won't have enough left to reach Europe. We'll have to let the balloon ride lower down."

"How far down do you want to go?" asked Max.

"Right to the sea if we have to," Ben replied.

Larry peered over the edge of the gondola to see how far they were from the clouds. What he saw astonished him. A huge round hole had opened in the clouds, and the balloon seemed to be plunging directly into it.

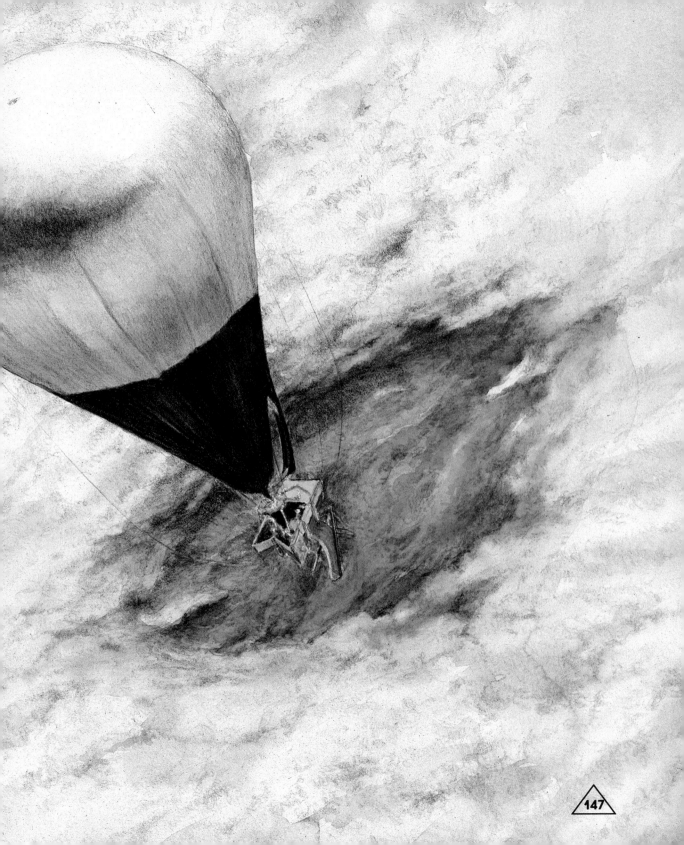

2

The flight of the *Double Eagle II* seemed doomed. The balloon was plummeting toward the sea, and the balloonists could spare no ballast to stop its fall. Larry kept calling out their altitude: 7,000 feet, 6,000 feet, 5,000 feet. At last, at 4,500 feet, the balloon stopped its descent.

"We're still in the clouds!" cried Larry, biting his lip nervously. He knew that if the winds carried the balloon under the clouds, where the sun couldn't shine on it, the flight was lost. They wouldn't be able to break through the clouds and climb back into the heat of the sun. Scarcely daring to breathe, Larry waited to see what would happen. The balloon continued to hang motionless in the sky.

The air was very warm, and suddenly Max understood what had happened. They had flown into a column of air warmer than the balloon. Like a cold, heavy weight, *Double Eagle II* had plunged through the warm air down toward the sea.

The three balloonists could hear waves pounding below them. "We're going to lose the flight," Larry said, almost angrily. "We've come all this way, and we're going to lose it."

There was nothing to do but wait. Feeling the warmth of the sun on his face, Ben gazed out at the milky white sky and the crisp line of the horizon that separated sea and sky. If the sun heated the helium and the balloon ascended, he knew they just might reach Europe. If not, the storm would surely engulf them, and the flight would be lost.

The sun kept shining on them steadily. At last the balloon began to ascend, rising very slowly at first but gathering speed as the air thinned. Soon the *Double Eagle II* had reached an altitude of 25,000 feet! Once again the three balloonists had a chance of reaching Europe.

Their supply of ballast, however, was very low. That afternoon, Ben, Max, and Larry began an exhausting task. They piled up everything they could afford to throw overboard—not only the remaining bags of sand but also dead batteries, surplus radios, their oxygen masks, a life raft, and even a parachute. When these items were gone, they would have nothing left to throw overboard except themselves. Ben knew that without more ballast they could stay up for only one more night. They had to reach Europe the next day—or not at all.

Suddenly, just before ten o'clock that night, Larry shouted, "Look, I see lights!"

Ben and Max jumped up, and in the distance they saw lamplight twinkling in dozens of cottage windows. When Larry tuned in the two-way radio, a flight controller said, "*Double Eagle II*, you have just crossed the coast of Ireland."

The skies above Ireland were cloudless. By the light of the full moon, Larry could see fields and winding limestone walls and even the emerald color of the grass two miles below. This moment of triumph was eerily quiet, interrupted only by the barking of the dogs in Ireland.

Now that the *Double Eagle II* had crossed the Atlantic Ocean, the balloonists had to decide whether they would land in England or France. England would be acceptable, but France would be better. To reach France, however, they would have to cross Ireland, Wales, England, and the English Channel. Could they keep the balloon in the air long enough?

At ten-thirty the next morning, the balloonists reached the coast of England and were greeted by a magical sight. On the ground, thousands of lights flickered from all directions. People in every city and village in southern England had come out to greet the American balloonists by flashing mirrors in the bright sunlight. From their gondola, the balloonists flashed a greeting back with their own small mirror.

The balloon was flying at almost 15,000 feet. The English Channel lay ahead, and beyond it lay their destination, France.

Ben and Max realized that by starting across the Channel they were taking a great risk. Their ballast was almost gone, so if they lost altitude over the Channel or if a stray wind flung them back to sea, they would be helpless. They would have to land in the water, and their flight wouldn't count as an Atlantic crossing.

The balloonists watched their instruments nervously as the *Double Eagle II* moved out over the water. They were traveling southeast, crossing the Channel on a diagonal. Below, Max could see smoke from freighters blowing in exactly the wrong direction—back toward England. For a time the balloon's flight paralleled the French coast, but at last the wind shifted, and at four-thirty in the afternoon the *Double Eagle II* crossed the coast of France.

Below, in the city of Le Havre, thousands of people thronged the streets to watch the balloon pass over them. Ben released some helium, and the balloon gradually descended. Floating over the fields and villages of France, Ben and Max began arguing about landing sites. The sun would set in one and a half hours, and Ben wanted to prolong the flight until the last possible moment. ''Why don't we land in that field?'' Max kept asking, but Ben, exhausted and irritated, kept refusing Max's suggestions.

Finally, with only half an hour of daylight left, Ben spied a field near a highway, just beyond a small village. ''All right,'' he said, ''we'll put it down.'' As he spoke the words, he was overwhelmed by sadness, knowing that the adventure was almost over.

Descending at 200 feet a minute, the *Double Eagle II* floated over the village of Miserey toward a field of ripe barley. For the first time the balloonists could see that the roads were crowded with cars. Planes and helicopters filled the sky, and hundreds of people ran across the fields to meet the balloon.

Ben kept his eyes on the ground, waiting until the balloon had cleared the power lines at the edge of the field. When he shouted, "Drop the ropes," the three balloonists threw the trail ropes over the side of the gondola. These ropes, dragging through the barley, helped pull the gondola down. Then, just as the gondola touched the soil, Ben yanked the rip line. Helium gushed out of the balloon, and the empty envelope slowly fluttered to the ground.

Within seconds of the landing, thousands of excited people swarmed over the field, cheering and laughing. They climbed into the gondola, slapping the balloonists' shoulders and trying to shake their hands. The balloonists had never dreamed of such a welcome. Police officers had to escort them through the jubilant crowd to a waiting helicopter.

Looking down at the noisy well-wishers, Ben, Max, and Larry realized that their feat was far more than a personal triumph. This crowd was paying homage to three men who had done the impossible. By crossing the Atlantic Ocean in a balloon, Ben Abruzzo, Max Anderson, and Larry Newman had taken their place in history.

154

1 Explain how Ben and Max fulfilled their dream.

2 What problems did Ben and Max face on their second flight?

3 If you had been Ben, would you have made the second flight? Explain your answer.

4 Writers keep readers interested by building suspense. How does the writer of this selection build suspense? Read the sentences or paragraphs that illustrate your answer.

5 Max said that flying across the Atlantic in a balloon had always seemed impossible. What do you think makes people want to do seemingly impossible things?

Bibliography

Balloons, Zeppelins, and Dirigibles by Acron Percefull. Watts. A history of hot-air balloons and other unusual aircraft.

Bag of Smoke by Lonzo Anderson. Knopf. Gives an account of the first experiment in flying a balloon voyage.

From Balloon Gondolas to Manned Spacecraft (film). NASA. Follows the history of people's efforts to travel through air and space.

who knows if the moon's

from *Tulip & Chimneys*

by E.E. Cummings

who knows if the moon's
a balloon, coming out of a keen city
in the sky—filled with pretty people?
(and if you and i should

get into it, if they
should take me and take you into their balloon,
why then
we'd go up higher with all the pretty people

than houses and steeples and clouds:
go sailing
away and away sailing into a keen
city which nobody's ever visited, where

always
       it's
              Spring) and everyone's
in love and flowers pick themselves

A DREAM TO RUN

by Beverly Ruuth

Chris dreams of running on the middle-school track team and being a star. But she has an obstacle in her way—she is nearly blind. How can a blind person run track?

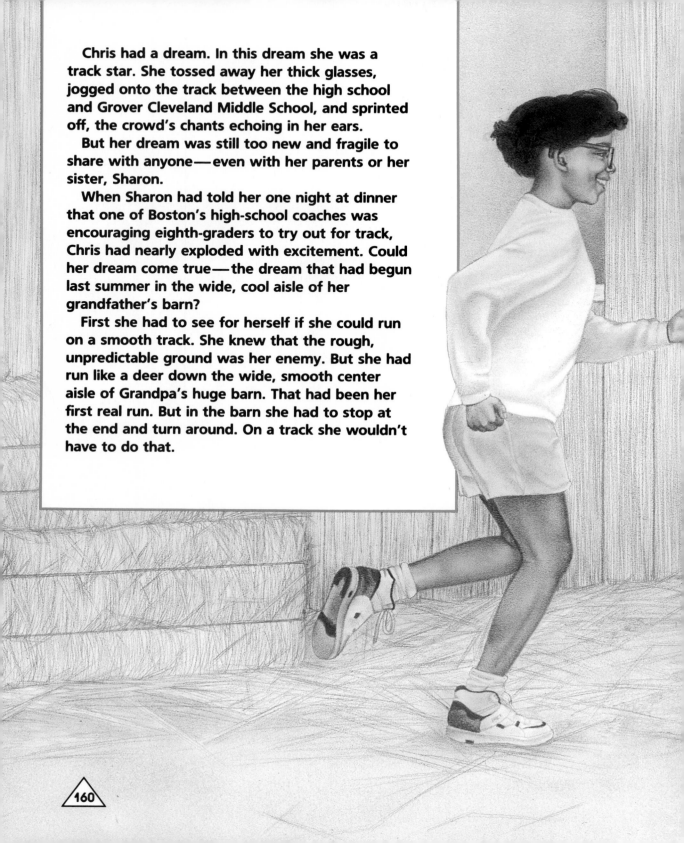

Chris had a dream. In this dream she was a track star. She tossed away her thick glasses, jogged onto the track between the high school and Grover Cleveland Middle School, and sprinted off, the crowd's chants echoing in her ears.

But her dream was still too new and fragile to share with anyone—even with her parents or her sister, Sharon.

When Sharon had told her one night at dinner that one of Boston's high-school coaches was encouraging eighth-graders to try out for track, Chris had nearly exploded with excitement. Could her dream come true—the dream that had begun last summer in the wide, cool aisle of her grandfather's barn?

First she had to see for herself if she could run on a smooth track. She knew that the rough, unpredictable ground was her enemy. But she had run like a deer down the wide, smooth center aisle of Grandpa's huge barn. That had been her first real run. But in the barn she had to stop at the end and turn around. On a track she wouldn't have to do that.

Chris was standing alone at the one busy intersection between her house and the two schools, listening to the roaring traffic and feeling the sucking wind of its frenzied passing.

She held her breath to listen more intently. The street finally grew quiet. No engine sounds, no wind grabbing at her gym shorts. As she dashed across the four lanes, the high-pitched whine of a small car far off in the distance broke the silence.

With the dangerous street behind her and the soft grass of the athletic field under her feet, Chris broke into a cautious trot. She squinted, trying to see the short white fence that marked the track. She still couldn't see it, but she knew where it was.

A minute later she touched the fence.

"Well, here you are," dream Chris said to real-life Chris. "What are you going to do now?"

Real-life Chris put her hands on her hips. "I'm going to walk it once around first," she said. "Then I'm going to run until . . . until I fall, probably."

It took forever to walk the track. Chris's feet seemed to have little springs under them that were coiled and ready to propel her forward. When she finally completed the course, she said to dream Chris, "See, no problem."

The little fence stood out, blurry but white against the green grass, and the track was a smooth brown ribbon in front of her. Without cracks, rocks, roots, or stray toys to trip her, Chris felt sure that she could do it.

Her heart nudged her throat. "This is it, Chris," she whispered. "Don't goof it." She positioned herself into an awkward crouch.

In her mind the starting gun sounded through the clean spring air, and she was off. Cheers rose all around her.

Her feet had wings. They touched the ground only briefly, setting up a rhythm for her breathing to match. Even her heart beat time to the rhythm her feet kept. She was flying, skimming the earth like a deer.

Oh, please don't fall, she begged herself. Her silent words fell into rhythm, too. No longer was she confined to a ten-foot radius of blurry obstacles she had to walk carefully around and through. She was completely free!

Her heart was ahead of her feet, and she didn't want to stop. She was ready to run to the end of the earth. But her body rebelled, and she began to slow down, still letting the momentum of the run carry her as far as it could.

"I . . . I did it!" she gasped. "I can run!" Joyfully, she leaped into thé air. "Do you hear that, world?" she cried. "I can run!"

"You sure can, young lady." The male voice startled her, and she jumped around. A tall, graying, dark-haired man in sweat pants came into view.

Before she had time to worry about talking to a strange man in a deserted athletic field, he said, "I'm Gus Silverton, the track coach here. And who, may I ask, are you?"

"I'm . . . I'm Chris Gillett. I'm in eighth grade at the middle school."

He was studying her very carefully. "I don't remember you trying out for track," he said finally.

"I didn't."

"Why?"

"Because I'm nearly blind and I wasn't sure that I could run. I mean, without running into things and falling."

"Well, you sure can, can't you?" he said. "This isn't official, but I'd say you ran the course in about sixty-eight seconds."

"Is that good?"

"Fifty-eight is state level. You're good, my girl, very good. Why, with a little training . . ."

"Oh, Coach Silverton!" She wanted to cry or hug him. "You mean even though I have poor vision, I could still enter state competition?"

"Sure, Chris. There are blind sprinters, skiers, swimmers, and ice skaters. Of course we'll have to talk to your doctor . . . and your parents."

"Oh, I know my doctor will be for it. He wants me to do everything I can. And my whole family is athletic, so I'm sure my parents will let me."

"Good." Coach Silverton patted her shoulder. "Bring your parents, if they can come, and meet me back here tomorrow at two o'clock."

That evening Chris discussed her dream with her family. Her parents were surprised. "*You* want to run?" her mother asked.

"Oh, yes!" Chris felt the power of her dream building. "Coach Silverton wants you and Daddy to meet him at the track tomorrow."

"Me, too," Sharon said. "If you're going to run, I've got to see it."

The next day her whole family met Coach Silverton. Sharon hugged her tight and told her to go for it. So did Mom. And even Dad looked hopeful.

Coach Silverton blew his little black whistle, and the starting gun went off in Chris's mind. Around the dirt track her long legs carried her like the wind.

"Come on, Chris!"

"Go, Chrissy!"

"Come on, honey!"

As she crossed the finish line, the applause rolled in a deafening wave across the grandstand. A gold cup was placed in her hands.

Dad had his arm across her shoulders, Mom and Sharon were hugging her, and Coach Silverton was shaking her hand, welcoming his new star to the track team.

Talk about it!

1 How does Chris fulfill her dream in spite of the limitations of being nearly blind?

2 At what point in the selection did you first think that Chris was going to succeed?

3 What is one quality Chris has that helps her realize her dream? How do you know she has that quality?

4 What do you think about the way Chris's family and Coach Silverton react to her dream?

5 "A disability is only a handicap if you let it interfere with your dreams." What does this statement mean? Would Chris agree with it? Explain your answer.

Bibliography

Sports for the Handicapped by Anne Allen. Walker. Short stories tell of the recreational activities and sports available to handicapped persons.

World of Sports for Girls by Gail Andersen Myers. Westminster. Discusses the ever-increasing opportunities for women in sports.

BOLD—Blind Outdoor Leisure Development (film). Crystal Productions. Shows blind people participating in outdoor sports such as rafting, jogging, skiing, horseback riding, and golf.

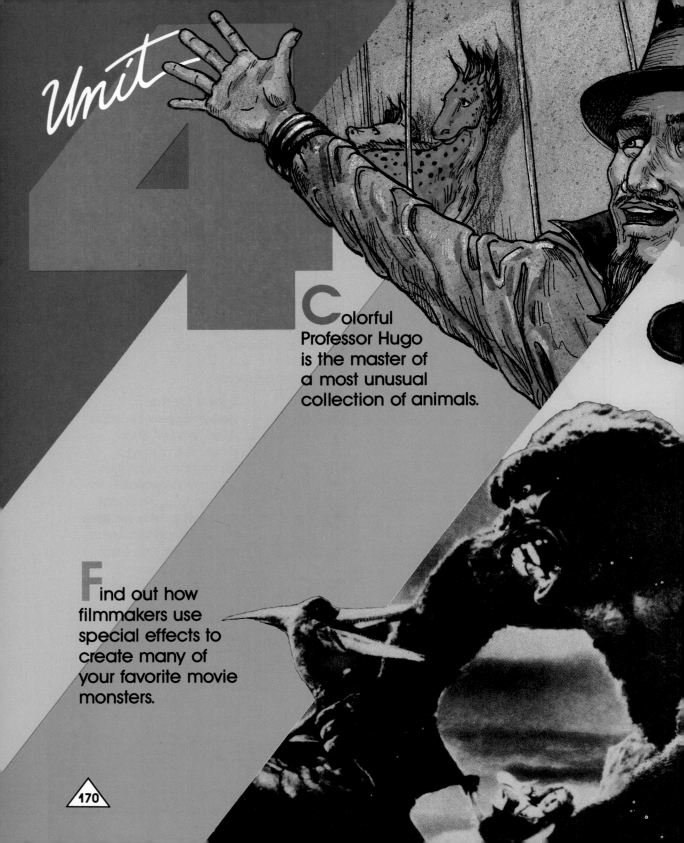

Unit

4

Colorful
Professor Hugo
is the master of
a most unusual
collection of animals.

Find out how
filmmakers use
special effects to
create many of
your favorite movie
monsters.

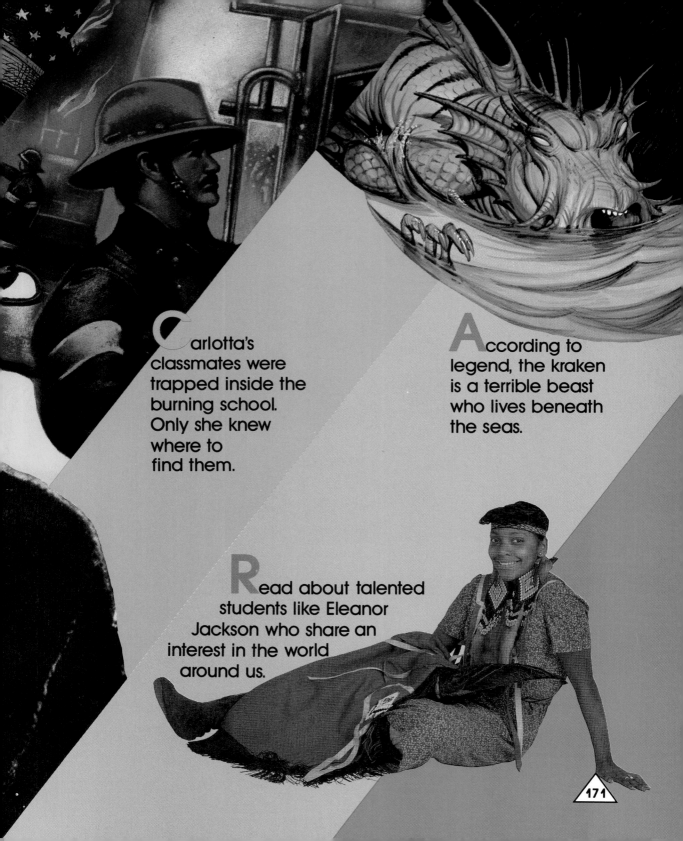

Carlotta's classmates were trapped inside the burning school. Only she knew where to find them.

According to legend, the kraken is a terrible beast who lives beneath the seas.

Read about talented students like Eleanor Jackson who share an interest in the world around us.

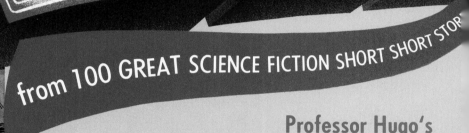

ZOO

from 100 GREAT SCIENCE FICTION SHORT SHORT STORIES

Professor Hugo's
Interplanetary Zoo is
unlike any other zoo.
What makes it so different?

by Edward D. Hoch

The children were always good during the month of August, especially when it began to get near the twenty-third. It was on this day that the great silver spaceship carrying Professor Hugo's Interplanetary Zoo settled down for its annual six-hour visit to the Chicago area.

Before daybreak the crowds would form, long lines of children and adults both, each one clutching his or her dollar, and waiting with wonderment to see what race of strange creatures the Professor had brought this year.

In the past they had sometimes been treated to three-legged creatures from Venus, or tall, thin men from Mars, or even snake-like horrors from somewhere more distant. This year, as the great round ship settled slowly to earth in the huge tri-city parking area just outside of Chicago, they watched with awe as the sides slowly slid up to reveal the familiar barred cages. In them were some wild breed of nightmare—small, horse-like animals that moved with quick, jerking motions and constantly chattered in a high-pitched tongue. The citizens of Earth clustered around as Professor Hugo's crew quickly collected the waiting dollars, and soon the good Professor himself made an appearance, wearing his many-colored rainbow cape and top hat. "Peoples of Earth," he called into his microphone.

The crowd's noise died down and he continued. "Peoples of Earth, this year you see a real treat for your single dollar—the little-known horse-spider people of Kaan—brought to you across a million miles of space at great expense. Gather around, see them, study them, listen to them, tell your friends about them. But hurry! My ship can remain here only six hours!"

And the crowds slowly filed by, at once horrified and fascinated by these strange creatures that looked like horses but ran up the walls of their cages like spiders. "This is certainly worth a dollar," one man remarked, hurrying away. "I'm going home to get my wife."

All day long it went like that, until ten thousand people had filed by the barred cages set into the side of the spaceship. Then, as the six-hour limit ran out, Professor Hugo once more took microphone in hand. "We must go now, but we will return next year on this day. And if you enjoyed our zoo this year, phone your friends in other cities about it. We will land in New York tomorrow, and next week on to London, Paris, Rome, Hong Kong, and Tokyo. Then on to other worlds!"

He waved farewell to them, and as the ship rose from the ground the Earth peoples agreed that this had been the very best Zoo yet. . . .

Some two months and three planets later, the silver ship of Professor Hugo settled at last onto the familiar jagged rocks of Kaan, and the queer horse-spider creatures filed quickly out

of their cages. Professor Hugo was there to say a few parting words, and then they scurried away in a hundred different directions, seeking their homes among the rocks.

In one, the she-creature was happy to see the return of her mate and offspring. She babbled a greeting in the strange tongue and hurried to embrace them. "It was a long time you were gone. Was it good?"

And the he-creature nodded. "The little one enjoyed it especially. We visited eight worlds and saw many things."

The little one ran up the wall of the cave. "On the place called Earth it was the best. The creatures there wear garments over their skins, and they walk on two legs."

"But isn't it dangerous?" asked the she-creature.

"No," her mate answered. "There are bars to protect us from them. We remain right in the ship. Next time you must come with us. It is well worth the nineteen commocs it costs."

And the little one nodded. "It was the very best Zoo ever. . . ."

Talk about it!

1 Why is this zoo different from other zoos?

2 How does Professor Hugo profit from the natural curiosity present in creatures of many worlds?

3 What is the surprising viewpoint revealed at the end of the selection? Do you like stories that end with surprising twists? Explain your answer.

4 What is the author trying to tell us about how we view the world?

Bibliography

Stranger from the Stars by Nancy Etchemendy. Avon. Ruthie helps a being from another world return home.

Aliens in the Family by Margaret Mahy. Scholastic. A New Zealand teenager feels she is being treated as an alien, until she meets a real alien.

Space Quest: The Sarien Encounter (Microcomputer program). Sierra. Play the role of Roger Wilco, a janitor who must defend his spaceship against alien invaders.

Beasts and ALIENS

by Michael Di Leo

Not all actors in the movies are alive. Some of them are made of rubber, metal, or plastic and play giant apes, space aliens, or other weird roles. How are these "actors" created?

Deep in a jungle, two beasts face each other, ready for battle. One is a dinosaur, its jaws stretched wide open, showing knifelike teeth. The other is a huge ape, its lips curled in a snarl.

Both animals are taller than the trees around them. Their battle is sure to trample this part of the jungle. Suddenly, however, a hand reaches down from above. It belongs to a man at least four times bigger than the animals. He lifts the ape right out of the jungle. Who could this enormous giant be?

Actually the man is no giant. His name is Willis O'Brien, and he is only about six feet tall. The ape in his grip is a small rubber model. The jungle is just a fake landscape built on a tabletop. The year is 1933, and Willis O'Brien is in his studio filming scenes for the movie *King Kong*.

THE GIANT APE OF WILLIS O'BRIEN

King Kong was among the first great "special effects" films. Special effects are tricks used to film scenes that can't be acted out or set up in real life. They are used to film such happenings as cities burning down, people flying through the air, and worlds blowing up. They are also used to create strange beings that don't exist in real life. *King Kong,* for example, starred an ape that appeared to be 24 feet tall.

The movie is about a group of people who sail to a faraway island to make a film. The island is full of strange beasts. A huge ape named King Kong captures one member of the group, a woman named Ann. The other group members, however, manage to rescue Ann and catch Kong. They take Kong to New York City in chains. The huge ape breaks looseand goes on a rampage. Finally, planes with guns shoot Kong down as the ape climbs the Empire State Building, at that time the world's tallest building.

Willis O'Brien created the action of the beasts in *King Kong* through a technique called stop-motion filming. He began by making small rubber models of Kong and the other beasts. The models had joints so that their arms and legs could be moved into any position. He set the models amid tiny scenery and filmed his scenes one frame at a time.

In one part, for example, O'Brien wanted to show Kong striking a dinosaur. He set the little rubber Kong in front of the dinosaur model and raised Kong's fist. Then he shot one frame of film. Next he moved Kong's fist a tiny bit forward. He shot another frame of film. Again and again he moved Kong's arm slightly forward, shooting one frame of each position. After 24 frames, Kong's fist was actually touching the dinosaur's jaw.

When the film was shown, those 24 frames flashed by in a single second. Kong's fist looked as if it had shot forward and hit the dinosaur. Out of 24 motionless shots, O'Brien had created one second of motion.

In fact, O'Brien created all the movements of his monsters in this way. He used stop-motion to show Kong doing such things as bounding through a jungle, wrestling a flying reptile, and smashing a train. Each scene took a great deal of time to make. Filming five minutes of action meant setting up 7,200 shots! The hard work paid off. Kong looked very real to audiences of the time.

O'Brien was a pioneer of stop-motion filmmaking, and *King Kong* was his masterpiece. People flocked to his studio after that movie to learn his methods. One of his best students was Ray Harryhausen. Harryhausen developed into a master of special effects in his own right. Some people consider his work even greater than O'Brien's.

THE CREATURES OF RAY HARRYHAUSEN

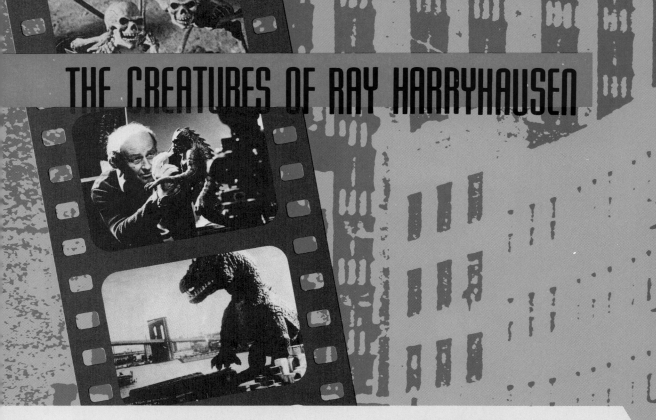

One of Harryhausen's first creatures was a giant dinosaur. It was seen in the 1953 movie *The Beast from 20,000 Fathoms.* One of his later creatures was the kraken. This beast, with four arms and a head like a lizard's, appeared in the 1982 film *The Clash of the Titans.* In between these films Harryhausen made all kinds of strange animals, from an octopus the size of a building to a flying monster called the Roc.

Some of Harryhausen's best special effects went into the 1963 movie *Jason and the Argonauts.* This movie was based on a Greek myth about a group of men searching for a magical object

called the Golden Fleece. The movie contains one of the most complicated stop-motion scenes ever filmed. It shows three men having a sword fight with seven living skeletons.

The skeletons, of course, were not real. They were small rubber models. Filming seven such models in stop-motion was hard enough. Each model had to be set in a new position 24 times for every second of film. Harryhausen faced another problem too. The models and actors had to appear together— but how could they? The actors had to be filmed in real motion. The models could only be filmed in stop-motion. Also, the models and

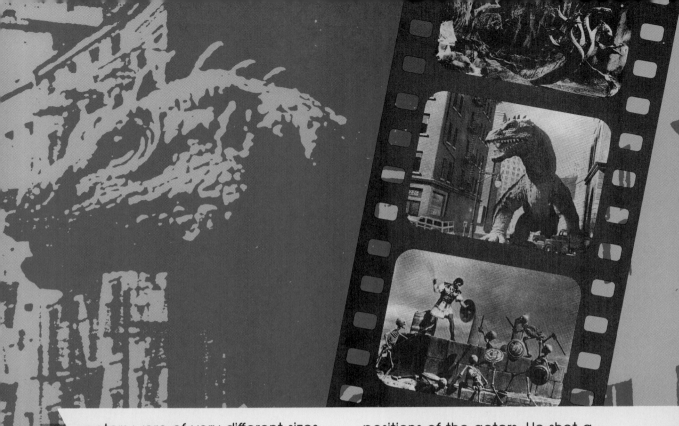

actors were of very different sizes.

Harryhausen met this problem by making a film of a film. First he filmed the live actors by themselves. He had them dash around the set, swinging their swords, fighting with thin air. He then projected this film one frame at a time onto a tiny screen. He placed the seven rubber skeletons in front of this screen. Skeletons and actors were now the same size and were facing each other. From the front, they looked as if they were in the same scene. Harryhausen shot one frame of this scene.

Then he switched to the next image on the tiny screen. He moved the skeletons to fit the new positions of the actors. He shot a frame of this new, slightly changed scene. Slowly, frame by frame, Harryhausen filmed the whole duel between skeletons and men. The duel lasted several minutes when it was shown in theaters. Those several minutes, however, took Harryhausen four-and-a-half months to film!

Harryhausen wasn't the only person making movies about strange creatures. Many filmmakers, however, didn't want to spend as much time and money as Harryhausen did. Since stop-motion filming can't be done quickly and cheaply, they looked for other ways to film fantastic creatures.

MONSTERS IN COSTUMES

The Japanese company Toho Studios found perhaps the simplest way of all. In 1954 the company produced a film called *Godzilla,* about a giant dinosaur. Toho's Godzilla was simply an actor in a rubber dinosaur suit. This monster looked fake, but the movie became popular anyway. Because of the success of *Godzilla,* Toho began to churn out monster movies by the dozen.

Of course, Toho had to invent more monsters. The movie *Godzilla* was followed by one that featured Rodan, a flying reptile with a 500-foot wingspan. Next came movies with a giant caterpillar, a dragon with three heads, a huge spider, and a giant snake. Toho even made a movie called *Hedorah the Smog Monster.*

When the Toho filmmakers ran out of ideas for new monsters, they teamed up the old ones. They made such films as *King Kong Versus Godzilla* and *Godzilla Versus the Smog Monster.* One film, *Destroy All Monsters,* has all the Toho monsters living together on a place called Monster Island. All the monsters, of course, were really actors wearing monster suits. Unfortunately, however, that is very much what they looked like.

Other filmmakers copied Toho, but they improved on Toho's methods. They made better costumes for their actors. They also tried another alternative to stop-motion filming. They built life-sized machines to play their creatures. Some machines were robots that could move on their own; others were operated with wires and strings, like puppets.

MACHINES IN THE MOVIES

Machines were easy to film. The hard part was building them. The first mechanical creatures could make only a few simple moves. The shark-shaped machine that was built for the 1975 movie *Jaws,* for example, could do only two things. It could swim, and it could open its deadly-looking jaws. That much was scary enough, though. This movie about a huge white shark that attacks swimmers near a popular beach frightened audiences all across the United States.

Then came the movie *Star Wars,* which presented whole new worlds of strange beings. Some of these beings were actually actors wearing costumes and makeup. Some beings were created through stop-motion filming of models. Others, however, such as the popular R2-D2, were played by machines. R2-D2 was a small, intelligent robot. Unlike most movie creatures of the past, R2-D2 was one of the heroes. It wasn't supposed to scare anyone. It was supposed to be cute and lovable.

At first glance, building a machine to play R2-D2 might seem easy. After all, R2-D2 was supposed to *be* a machine. What's more, it looked about as simple as a tin can on wheels. However, this simple-looking machine had a complicated job. It had to roll at many different speeds, turn corners, whistle, squeak, rotate its head, and stick little levers out of its body. All these moves had to be timed just right. R2-D2 had to look as if it were reacting to the other characters.

Filmmaker George Lucas had two models of R2-D2 built. One model had room inside for a small person to work the robot. This model, however, tipped over easily when the person inside it tried to walk.

Lucas therefore had his workers build a radio-controlled model. It was used in shots of R2-D2 moving fast. Controlling the machine by radio, however, was not easy. Many times R2-D2 bumped into furniture, people, and walls. Sometimes it tipped over as it turned a corner too fast. When R2-D2 finally appeared on the screen, though, audiences were delighted. For many people, it was the ultimate special effect—a machine with a personality.

Perhaps partly because of R2-D2's success, more movies about friendly robots soon appeared. A robot called Johnny Five was the star of a movie called *Short Circuit* and its sequel, *Short Circuit 2.* In both movies, Johnny Five was run by a kind of remote control. A "roboteer" wore a suit with special controls. Every time the roboteer moved in the suit, the suit sent a radio message to the robot to move in exactly the same way. In *Short Circuit 2,* released in 1987, Johnny Five could bend, turn, pick things up, and even bat its eyelashes.

A few years after *Star Wars,* Steven Spielberg, the director of *Jaws,* made a movie called *E.T.: The Extraterrestrial.* It starred a mechanical character even more amazing than R2-D2 and Johnny Five: the little space alien known as E.T.

Spielberg's first problem was deciding how E.T. should look. In most previous movies, space aliens had looked like scary monsters. Spielberg wanted E.T. to look weird but not scary. He wanted viewers to end up loving E.T., just as the young boy Elliot did in the movie. He hired Carlo Rimbaldi, an artist, to design the alien.

Spielberg had to have several models built to handle all of E.T.'s movements. One model was hollow and had a small person inside.

It was like a costume. This model was used only a few times, in shots of E.T. walking around. Another E.T. was a lightweight machine that was loaded with wires and cables. It could make 86 different motions. It could even smile and make faces. It was perhaps the most complex mechanical creature ever built.

193

COMPUTER-GENERATED CHARACTERS

Spielberg set a different challenge for special-effects crews in the 1985 movie *Young Sherlock Holmes*. This time they had to make a "monster" that wasn't really there at all. In one scene of the movie, a knight pictured in a stained-glass window in a church suddenly seems to come alive. He leaps from the window, waving his sword, and terrifies a watching priest.

The knight couldn't be a puppet or a machine, Spielberg decided. He shouldn't be like R2-D2, either. He had to look as if he were still made of pieces of glass, even when he was moving. Flames of the candles in the church should shine through his body. And he and the priest had to be seen on the screen together.

The stained-glass knight was made by a computer—with a lot of hard work. First, an actual stained-glass model of the knight was made. Then the designers traced the model with a "digitizing wand," which gives a computer detailed information about the shapes of objects. Information from the wand was then fed into a special computer called a Pixar Image Computer.

The Pixar made a sketch of the knight. Special-effects artists then began to make the drawing look like glass. At first the glass seemed too clean. The artists had to write computer programs that added smudges to make the glass look old. They also had to write computer programs to make the knight move. When completed, the image of the knight could move in 280 different ways.

Finally the priest and the knight had to be put together. The actor playing the priest was filmed in the church. Then the special-effects team ran the film past a laser scanner. The special laser light allowed the filmed images to be turned into a form that the Pixar could "understand." Later, the laser turned the images of the priest and the knight back into filmed form. It was the first time a figure made by a computer had appeared against a real background along with a real actor. And the stained-glass knight was on the screen for only 38 seconds!

Outrageous creatures are no longer simply something strange to be glimpsed on a movie screen. Instead, they seem real and ordinary enough to be part of everyday life.

Talk about it!

1 Describe the methods that filmmakers use to create strange beings that don't exist in real life.

2 What did you learn about special effects in movies that you didn't know before reading this selection?

3 How did the subheadings help you read and understand the selection?

4 Which method for creating strange creatures did you find most interesting? Explain your answer.

5 What qualities and talents do people who create special effects have in common?

Bibliography

Lights! Camera! Scream! How to Make Your Own Monster Movies by Stephen Mooser. Messner. Use special effects to make your own science fiction films.

Science Fiction's Greatest Monsters by Daniel Cohen. Dodd, Mead. Memorable monsters from radio and television.

SPFX — The Making of "The Empire Strikes Back" (videocassette). Films Incorporated. Explores the art of creating illusions on film. Includes scenes from several movies.

THE KRAKEN

by Jack Prelutsky

Deep beneath the foaming billows
something's suddenly amiss
as a creature wakes from slumber
in the bottomless abyss,
and a panic fills the ocean,
every fish in frenzy flees
for the kraken has awakened
at the bottom of the seas.

It rises to the surface
with an overwhelming noise
and it hunts for mighty vessels
which it crushes and destroys,
then it chokes a great leviathan
with one stupendous squeeze—
oh the kraken has awakened
at the bottom of the seas.

How it lashes, how it thrashes,
how it flashes, how it flails,
how it dwarfs the greatest fishes,
even dwarfs the mighty whales!
Nothing living in the ocean
can enjoy a moment's ease
for the kraken has awakened
at the bottom of the seas.

199

A raging fire had trapped a teacher and his class somewhere in the school basement. Only Carlotta knew where they were—but she couldn't make anyone else understand!

How could she help them escape?

*O*UT OF THE

SILENCE

by Raboo Rodgers

The police had moved quickly to block off the school grounds. Carlotta stood across the street with the other students, watching in disbelief as the fire department desperately fought the fire. The situation looked hopeless. Heavy smoke billowed from every opening in the old school building, and flames licked out the windows. Suddenly the whole east end of the building exploded into flames. The noise was so loud that even Carlotta, as she adjusted the volume on her hearing aid, could hear a faint crackling and a muffled roar.

Across the street on the school grounds, Mr. MacIntire, the principal, was shouting in desperation to the fire chief. Carlotta read his lips, missing some of what he said because of the distance but seeing more than enough to understand. ". . . eight students and a teacher . . . in a basement room . . . trapped!"

The fire chief shook his head helplessly. Three times already fire fighters had tried to enter the building, only to be driven back by the intense heat and smoke. Now there was no hope at all. Carlotta saw the helplessness in the fire chief's face.

Carlotta's advanced physics class was trapped in the basement, and she should have been with them. She had stopped in the upstairs hall, however, to talk to Mr. MacIntire about her Phonic Ear. The Ear hung from Carlotta's neck and plugged into her hearing aid.

The Phonic Ear was a small radio receiver that received and amplified signals from a transmitter worn by her teachers. Born with a hearing impairment, Carlotta had been at a disadvantage in her classes. She was a good lip-reader, but lipreading wasn't 100 percent effective. Making good grades had been a struggle for her until she began to use the Phonic Ear.

Now Carlotta heard everything her teachers said, and her grades shot up. This year she was enrolled in the advanced physics class, the only class still held in any of the basement classrooms of the old school. That part of the school was being renovated.

A new wing was being added to the school. Heavy equipment—bulldozers and backhoes—had been digging the new foundation. Their weight had broken a natural-gas line leading into the basement, causing an explosion.

Carlotta had just turned away from Mr. MacIntire when the school building was rocked by the powerful blast. Smoke and debris burst from the basement stairwell, followed quickly by fire. Everyone on the upper two floors had gotten out, but no one in the basement had been able to escape.

Numbed, Carlotta now stood across the street and watched the school being consumed by fire. She wanted desperately to help but didn't know what she could possibly do. She idly turned up the volume on the Phonic Ear, then turned it down, then up again, listening to the rise and fall of static. Then, suddenly, with the volume up high she thought she heard a faint voice.

"Lie down . . . flat . . ."

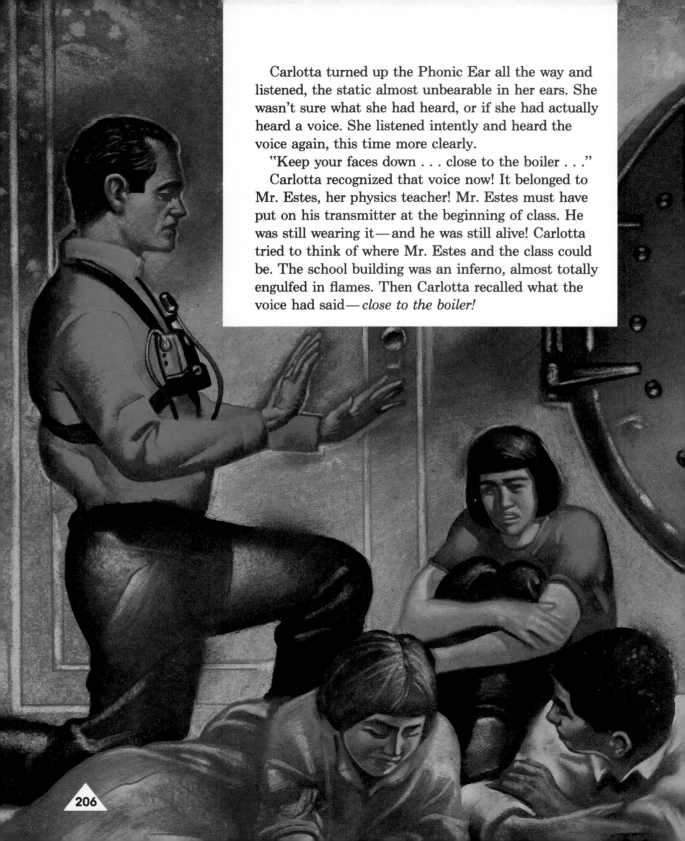

Carlotta turned up the Phonic Ear all the way and listened, the static almost unbearable in her ears. She wasn't sure what she had heard, or if she had actually heard a voice. She listened intently and heard the voice again, this time more clearly.

"Keep your faces down . . . close to the boiler . . ."

Carlotta recognized that voice now! It belonged to Mr. Estes, her physics teacher! Mr. Estes must have put on his transmitter at the beginning of class. He was still wearing it—and he was still alive! Carlotta tried to think of where Mr. Estes and the class could be. The school building was an inferno, almost totally engulfed in flames. Then Carlotta recalled what the voice had said—*close to the boiler!*

At one end of the basement was an old, unused boiler room. It was windowless and with its door closed would be sealed practically airtight. Carlotta thought that Mr. Estes and the class probably were in there, lying flat on the floor next to the old boiler, breathing in the last remaining pocket of air.

Carlotta bolted from the crowd and raced across the street to the school grounds, looking for the fire chief. Before she could locate him, two police officers stopped her.

"They're alive!" she shouted at them. "They're in the boiler room!"

The police officers just looked at Carlotta, their faces expressing concern and sympathy, but they hadn't understood her. Carlotta knew immediately what was wrong. Since she had been born with a hearing impairment, her speech had not developed the clarity of that of a person with normal hearing. Her speaking ability had improved with training over the years, but people who had never heard her speak often had difficulty understanding her.

Carlotta tried to speak more slowly, more distinctly. "They are in the boiler room! They are alive!"

All the police officers understood was that she was upset. "We know they're your friends, but there's nothing you can do. Please go back across the street," one of them said, gently pushing Carlotta back to the crowd.

Carlotta ran the length of the school building, weaving through the crowd, frantically searching for Mr. MacIntire or another teacher. Through the Phonic Ear she heard, "Stay calm . . . they'll be rescuing us any minute."

Mr. Estes's confidence made Carlotta shiver. She knew they probably *weren't* going to be rescued. All the entrances into the building were blocked by fire, and the police weren't able to understand her. She had to do something—anything—to help.

As flames began to break through the roof, Carlotta noticed a small bulldozer across the street at the edge of the excavation. Its engine had been left running, and Carlotta saw the bursts of smoke from its exhaust pipe as it idled.

Through the Phonic Ear, she heard Mr. Estes say, "Stay calm. Keep your head down!"

Carlotta began to run toward the bulldozer. She heard shouts and caught a glimpse of two police officers chasing her. She kept running, determined to help her doomed class. In seconds she reached the bulldozer and leaped into the driver's seat. Searching the controls, Carlotta found the throttle and pushed it to "full." The bulldozer roared forward, and she steered it down into the excavation.

The excavation sloped down toward the foundation of the school at the basement level. With the flames roaring overhead, Carlotta headed the bulldozer to the corner of the foundation. She rammed the machine into the building, knocking out blocks and making a hole.

Jumping from the bulldozer, Carlotta scrambled up over the blocks into the hole in the building. Air rushed into the opening with her. As she dropped down into the end of the hallway, she saw flames begin to reach toward the new draft she had made. Across the hall, less than ten feet away, was the door to the boiler room. She raced to the door and planted her shoulder firmly into it, pushing with all her strength. The door burst open, and Carlotta rushed into the room. Her classmates were lying face down on the floor.

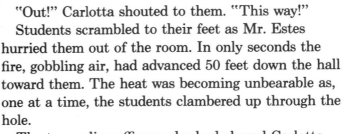

"Out!" Carlotta shouted to them. "This way!"

Students scrambled to their feet as Mr. Estes hurried them out of the room. In only seconds the fire, gobbling air, had advanced 50 feet down the hall toward them. The heat was becoming unbearable as, one at a time, the students clambered up through the hole.

The two police officers who had chased Carlotta stood outside and plucked the students out, sending them running up the slope of the excavation. Mr. Estes climbed out last. As he and the two officers scrambled up the slope, behind the students, fire exploded from the hole. Safely away from the fire, the exhausted group stopped to rest. The crowd across the street sent up a cheer.

Mr. Estes turned to Carlotta. "I kept telling everyone to stay calm," he said, "but I really didn't think we had a chance! How did you know where we were?"

Carlotta pointed to the transmitter that still hung from her physics teacher's neck.

Smiling, she replied, "Somebody put a bug in my ear."

Talk about it!

1 What does Carlotta do when she can't make anyone understand what she is saying about the trapped class?

2 Do you think Carlotta did all she could to make the police officers understand her? What do you think of the police officers' reaction to her? Explain your answer.

3 This story is told from Carlotta's point of view. Retell the story from another class member's point of view.

4 When did you first realize that Carlotta's Phonic Ear would be the key to the students' escape?

5 The word *bug* can be used to refer to a listening device or to a hint or suggestion about something. How does Carlotta's closing comment, "Somebody put a bug in my ear," refer to both meanings?

Bibliography

A Dance to Still Music *by Barbara Corcoran. Atheneum.* Margaret must learn to adjust to her deafness.

Triumph! Conquering Your Physical Disability *by Le Roy Hagman. Messner.* Survival skills and tips for disabled persons.

Deaf Like Me *(videocassette). Barr.* A deaf girl is fascinated by a mime who performs at her school. Later, she learns that the performer is also deaf.

THE WO

R L D

AROUND US

These three students appreciate
very different aspects of the
world around them. How do their
interests and feelings affect their
lives?

LINDSAY PETERSON
Rogers Middle School

Ribbons

My friends are many colored
ribbons
They decorate my life
They always bring sunshine
Happiness comes with them, too
Filling my world with many
Colors and
Life.

People ask me where the ideas for my poems come from. They come from thinking about and visualizing things. "Ribbons" came from a picture in my head of different colored ribbons. As I thought about the picture, it began to remind me of all the people of different colors I know. It seemed like a perfect poem to submit for the Racial and Ethnic Harmony Contest that was held when I was in fifth grade.

I started writing when I was in second grade. I won four tickets to the Edaville Railroad for one of my pieces. I continued writing through elementary school. I did not realize when I submitted "Ribbons" in fifth grade that my poem and I would wind up on TV.

I was very excited when I found out that I was one of the contest winners, and that "Ribbons" was going to be seen on TV. I was nervous, though, about making the TV spot. It took a whole day to film it. I had to lie on a rug, writing my poem down on a piece of paper. Then I looked up and said "Ribbons" as though I had just thought of the title. Then ribbons with faces of kids behind them flowed through the air.

215

DAVID WILSON
Edwards Middle School

Some people give you strange looks when you tell them that you collect snakes for a hobby. I think that collecting them and observing them is fascinating.

I started collecting snakes when I was nine years old. I was on vacation that summer with my grandfather. We were looking for worms in the woods. As we were looking, I saw a garden snake. When I tried to pick it up, it struck at me. I was finally able to pick it up with a stick. This was the beginning of my fascination with snakes.

When I turned 12, I was becoming more and more interested in snakes and their behavior. I wondered how they got their prey and how they digested their food. As I collected snakes, I began to understand more about how they killed their prey. I was able to observe them digesting their food. I started noticing the differences in their shapes and movements.

I have owned 14 snakes, among them a rattler, a cobra, a sidewinder, a baby boa constrictor, and several garden snakes. But I still have a great deal to learn. I've noticed that some of my snakes do not do well. I found out that some of them need to live in the water.

Keeping snakes has its problems, too. For instance, there was the time that six of them got loose in the house. I had the hardest time finding the one curled up in a corner!

I've learned many things about snakes in the past few years. I've learned the proper ways to feed and handle them. Perhaps the most important thing I've learned is to devote the time it takes to keep pets healthy and in good shape.

Even though my name is Eleanor Jackson, I am also known as Indian Dancer. I am a Wampanoag[1] Indian. My people call me Indian Dancer because I love to dance.

I am very proud of my Indian ancestry. To honor my people, I observe our customs and participate in many ceremonies. Since my people do not believe in drugs, alcohol, or evil deeds, I keep these things out of my own life. The Wampanoag treat other tribes and other races equally. I believe in this as well.

To bring honor to my people, I participate in many contests. Dancing is my specialty, but I also compete in contests that are judged on the way you act towards other people.

Dancing is an important part of my life. I dance at many socials and powwows all over New England. I know many dances, but my favorite is the crow hop dance. I was honored to be the first girl to do the feather dance, a dance usually done by men and boys.

[1]Wampanoag [wom•pə•nō′ag]

The costumes for Indian dances are very important because the appearance or color of each item of clothing has meaning. I make my own costumes, except for the shell and stone beads made by my grandmother.

I love attending the seasonal powwows. Over 3,000 people attend the summer powwow. I make beads and sell them there. We eat lots of great seafood and foods from the Earth.

Although I live in the city, I don't feel all that comfortable here. I would rather live in the woods. I attend a survival camp in the summer where we learn how to fish, make natural medicines, track animals, and find food.

I write poetry and I am very interested in the interpretation of dreams. When I grow up, I hope to be a model. I will start modeling classes soon. I would like to study the history of my people and participate in our struggle to keep our land. No matter what else I do in the future, my people will always be important in my life.

Talk about it!

1 How are the lives of Lindsay, David, and Eleanor affected by their appreciation of the world around them?

2 What qualities do Lindsay, David, and Eleanor share?

3 What does Eleanor Jackson mean when she says, "My people will always be important in my life"? Explain your answer.

4 Which of the three young people would you enjoy knowing? Explain your answer.

Bibliography

Cry from the Earth; Music of the North American Indians by John Biehorst. Four Winds/Macmillan. Native American music, dances, and instruments are described.

Bring Me All Your Dreams selected by Nancy Larrick. Evans. This collection includes favorite poems about dreams by "dreamers" from around the world.

Circle of Songs (videocassette). Great Plains. Demonstrates the songs and dances of several Indian tribes.

Glossary

The glossary is a special dictionary for this book. The glossary tells you how to spell a word, how to pronounce it, and what the word means.

A blue triangle ▲ at the end of the entry tells you that an illustration is given for that word.

The following abbreviations are used throughout the glossary: *n.*, noun; *v.*, verb; *adj.*, adjective; *adv.*, adverb; *pl.*, plural; *syn.*, synonym; *syns.*, synonyms.

An accent mark (/) is used to show which syllable receives the most stress. For example, in the word *granite* [gran/ it], the first syllable receives more stress. Sometimes in words of three or more syllables, there is also a lighter mark to show that a syllable receives a lighter stress. For example, in the word *helicopter* [hel/ ə • kop/ tər], the first syllable has the most stress, and the third syllable has lighter stress.

The symbols used to show how each word is pronounced are explained in the "Pronunciation Key" on the next page.

a	add, map	m	move, seem	u	up, done
ā	ace, rate	n	nice, tin	û(r)	burn, term
â(r)	care, air	ng	ring, song	y͞o͞o	fuse, few
ä	palm, father	o	odd, hot	v	vain, eve
b	bat, rub	ō	open, so	w	win, away
ch	check, catch	ô	order, jaw	y	yet, yearn
d	dog, rod	oi	oil, boy	z	zest, muse
e	end, pet	ou	pout, now	zh	vision, pleasure
ē	equal, tree	o͞o	took, full	ə	the schwa,
f	fit, half	o͞o	pool, food		an unstressed
g	go, log	p	pit, stop		vowel representing
h	hope, hate	r	run, poor		the sound spelled
i	it, give	s	see, pass		a in *above*
ī	ice, write	sh	sure, rush		e in *sicken*
j	joy, ledge	t	talk, sit		i in *possible*
k	cool, take	th	thin, both		o in *melon*
l	look, rule	t̶h̶	this, bathe		u in *circus*

A

a·dept [ə·dept′] *adj.* Highly skilled or well-trained. She will probably win a basketball scholarship because she is such an *adept* player. *syn.* capable

aisle [īl] *n.* A passageway, such as one in a theater, that separates one section of seats from another. The movie was so sad that people were crying as they walked up the *aisle* toward the exit. *syn.* passage ▲

am·pli·fy [am′plə·fī] *v.* **am·pli·fied, am·pli·fy·ing** To increase in power or capacity. This machine can *amplify* sounds in nature that you could not ordinarily hear. *syn.* expand

an·nu·al [an′yoo·əl] *adj.* Coming or happening once each year. On July 4 our city holds its *annual* parade to honor the United States. *syn.* yearly

a·rouse [ə·rouz′] *v.* **a·roused, a·rous·ing** To stir up; awaken. You may *arouse* your sister's suspicion about the surprise party if you make a lot of phone calls from home.

as·cer·tain [as′ər·tān′] *v.* **as·cer·tained, as·cer·tain·ing** To find out for certain; make sure of. Amanda tried to *ascertain* what the book was about by examining its table of contents.

awe [ô] *n.* A feeling of fear and wonder, as at the size, power, or majesty of something. Tourists stare in *awe* at the height of the buildings in Chicago. *syn.* amazement

B

baf·fle [baf′əl] *v.* **baf·fled, baf·fling** To confuse; bewilder; perplex. The causes of many deadly diseases continue to *baffle* scientists. *syns.* mystify, puzzle

bal·last [bal′əst] *n.* Anything heavy, as sand, stone, or water, carried on a ship or balloon to steady it. The balloon pilot unloaded some *ballast* so that the balloon could rise higher. ▲

bam·boo·zle [bam·boo′zəl] *v.* **bam·boo·zled, bam·boo·zling** To trick; cheat. He tried to *bamboozle* the public by selling pieces of land that were already owned by the government. *syn.* swindle

C

clar•i•ty [klar′ə•tē] *n.* Clearness. The *clarity* of the water allowed me to see the shells on the bottom.

col•umn [kol′əm] *n.* A tall post or a pillar shaped like a cylinder, such as used to support a building. The porch roof was supported by a *column* at each corner. ▲

com•pli•cat•ed [kom′plə•kā′tid] *adj.* Difficult because of many steps or details involved. I had to ask my math teacher how to begin the *complicated* word problem. *syn.* complex

com•put•er-gen•er•at•ed [kəm•pyoo′tər jen′ə•rā′təd] *adj.* Produced or caused by a computer. Using *computer-generated* art in that booklet means that we will not have to draw all of the art by hand.

con•fine [kən•fīn′] *v.* **con•fined, con•fin•ing** To shut in or keep shut in. The doctor says that she must *confine* me to bed while I am recovering from the flu. *syn.* limit

con•sole [kən•sōl′] *v.* **con•soled, con•sol•ing** To comfort in sorrow or disappointment. Yolanda was very sad when her dog got lost, so I tried to *console* her by letting her play with my dog. *syn.* cheer

cou•ri•er [koor′ē•ər] *n.* A messenger who delivers important messages or packages, often with great speed. The *courier* brought Isaac an important package from the airport. *syn.* carrier

cov•er [kuv′ər] *n.* A disguise used to protect or hide a secret agent. Her job as a translator was only a *cover* for her spying operations. *syn.* camouflage

D

des•per•a•tion [des′pə•rā′shən] *n.* A state of anxiety that sometimes causes reckless behavior. In *desperation,* the woman went to every house in the neighborhood trying to find her lost cat. *syn.* hopelessness

die•sel [dē′zəl] *n.* A short form for *diesel fuel,* which is a heavy mineral oil used as fuel in some engines. All along the busy highway, you could smell the *diesel* from the trucks that traveled the road.

a	add	o	odd	oi	oil
ā	ace	ō	open	ou	pout
â	care	ô	order	ng	ring
ä	palm	o͞o	took	th	thin
e	end	o͞o	pool	th	this
ē	equal	u	up	zh	vision
i	it	û	burn		
ī	ice	yo͞o	fuse		

ə = { a in *above*   e in *sicken*   i in *possible*
     o in *melon*   u in *circus* }

dig•it [dij′it] *n.* A numeral from 0 to 9. Write clearly each *digit* of the answer to the math problem. *syn.* number

di•lap•i•dat•ed [di•lap′ə•dā′tid] *adj.* Falling to pieces. The city should knock down that *dilapidated* building before it falls and hurts someone. *syn.* decayed

di•vert [dī•vûrt′] *v.* **di•vert•ed, di•vert•ing**   To turn aside. No one was able to *divert* Dennis from his goal of writing a play. *syns.* change, detour

draft•ing [draft′ing] *n.* Informal for *mechanical drawing.* Tyrone will study *drafting* in mechanical drawing class so that he can prepare accurate blueprints for buildings.

drudg•er•y [druj′ər•ē] *n.* Dull, hard, unpleasant work. Some people don't mind the *drudgery* of housework because they like having clean homes.

du•el [d(y)o͞o′əl] *n.* Any conflict or contest between two individuals or forces. Long ago, arguments between people were sometimes settled by a *duel* with swords. ▲

E

em•brace [im•brās′] *v.* **em•braced, em•brac•ing**   To clasp or enfold in the arms; hug. Mother ran to *embrace* my brother when he came off the plane after his first three months in the army.

ep•i•lep•tic sei•zure [ep′ə•lep′tik sē′zhər] *n.* A sudden attack caused by a disorder of the nervous system. One of my classmates had an *epileptic seizure* that made his body move about wildly until after the nurse gave him some medicine.

es•pi•o•nage [es′pē•ə•nazh′] *n.* The act of spying. During an act of *espionage,* it is important to be alert for danger at all times.

ex•ca•va•tion [eks′kə•vā′shən] *n.* A pit or hollow made by digging; a dug-out area. Wooden walls were built to keep people away from the dangerous *excavation. syn.* hole ▲

F

fath•om [fath'əm] *v.* **fath•omed, fath•om•ing** To understand; figure out. I can't *fathom* why anyone would pollute the environment on purpose. *syn.* comprehend

fier•y [fir'ē] *n.* Full of feeling or passion. Sometimes his *fiery* temper caused him to become very angry over the smallest of matters. *syn.* intense

fil•a•ment [fil'ə•mənt] *n.* A very thin, threadlike structure such as the wire that produces light inside an electric light bulb. The light bulb did not work because the *filament* had broken. ▲

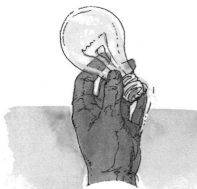

flu•o•res•cent [floo'ə•res'ənt] *adj.* Giving off light when acted upon by certain forms of energy, as by ultraviolet rays. My white clothing seemed to glow when I walked under the *fluorescent* light.

for•ti•fi•ca•tion [fôr'tə•fə•kā'shən] *n.* A place built for defense. The *fortification* built by the army could withstand almost any kind of attack from the enemy. *syn.* fort

frame [frām] *n.* One of a series of still pictures that makes up a motion-picture film. By looking separately at each *frame* of the movie, you can see the positions of the karate expert's arms and legs. ▲

fren•zied [fren'zēd] *adj.* Madly excited; wild. The *frenzied* cheering of the crowd encouraged the runners to go even faster. *syns.* confused, frantic

frost•bit•ten [frôst'bit•ən] *adj.* Injured (some part of the body) by exposure to freezing temperatures. Nina wore gloves to protect her already *frostbitten* fingers from the icy winds.

a	add	o	odd	oi	oil
ā	ace	ō	open	ou	pout
â	care	ô	order	ng	ring
ä	palm	o͞o	took	th	thin
e	end	o͞o	pool	th	this
ē	equal	u	up	zh	vision
i	it	û	burn		
ī	ice	yo͞o	fuse		

ə = { a in *above*   e in *sicken*   i in *possible*
      { o in *melon*   u in *circus*

227

G

gar·ment [gär′mənt] *n.* An article of clothing. Sean carefully laid each *garment* on his bed as he prepared to dress.

gon·do·la [gon′də·lə] *n.* A basket or enclosure suspended from a balloon. As we watched the balloon descend, we could see the faces of the people who stood in the *gondola.* ▲

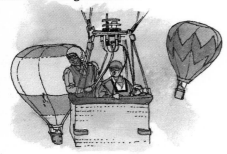

I

i·dly [īd′lē] *adv.* In a useless or meaningless way. While I read the book, I *idly* tapped a pencil on my desk.

im·pair·ment [im·pâr′mənt] *n.* Disability or limitation. Matthew did not let his sight *impairment* prevent him from working toward his goals.

im·pos·tor [im·pos′tər] *n.* A person who deceives, especially one who pretends to be someone else. The person on stage looked like the famous rock star, but he was really an *impostor.* *syn.* pretender

in·ad·e·quate [in·ad′ə·kwit] *adj.* Less than is needed or required. After I failed the test, Mother asked me to give a better explanation than the *inadequate* one I had given.

in·dus·tri·ous [in·dus′trē·əs] *adj.* Hardworking and energetic. Pablo was *industrious* Friday night and completed all of his homework. *syns.* busy, diligent

in·fer·no [in·fûr′nō] *n.* A place full of fire and intense heat. The inside of the burning building was an *inferno.* ▲

in·ter·cept [in′tər·sept′] *v.* **in·ter·cept·ed, in·ter·cept·ing** To keep something or someone from reaching a planned destination. I didn't want anyone to *intercept* the private message, so I delivered the envelope in person.

in·ter·plan·e·tar·y [in′tər·plan′ə·ter′ē] *adj.* Between or among planets. The first *interplanetary* spaceship that carries people will probably travel from Earth to Mars.

in·ter·sec·tion [in′tər·sek′shən] *n.* A crossing, especially a place where streets cross. It is important to look carefully in both directions before crossing that busy *intersection.*

in•trigue [in•trēg′] *n.* Sly, secret scheming or plotting. The tale of *intrigue* had us sitting on the edge of our seats, waiting to hear the outcome.

ma•nip•u•late [mə•nip′yə•lāt′] *v.* **ma•nip•u•lat•ed, ma•nip•u•lat•ing** To operate or work with the hands. Learning to *manipulate* all the controls in a car is an important part of learning to drive. *syn.* handle

mo•men•tous [mō•men′təs] *adj.* Very important. The founding of our city was a *momentous* event in our state's history. *syns.* great, major

ob•sta•cle [ob′stə•kəl] *n.* Something that stands in the way or interferes. That tall fence is an *obstacle* to my cutting across the schoolyard. *syns.* hindrance, obstruction ▲

oc•cu•py [ok′yə•pī′] *v.* **oc•cu•pied, oc•cu•py•ing** Taken and held possession of, as in war. The people of our country will fight against any nation that tries to *occupy* our land.

op•ti•mis•tic [op′tə•mis′tik] *adj.* Full of hope and cheerfulness. Ishmael is *optimistic* about our chances to win the soccer game tonight. *syns.* cheerful, hopeful

pat•ent [pat′(ə)nt] *n.* A government document giving an inventor the sole right to make and sell a new invention for a certain term of years. Uncle Julio applied for a *patent* for a new type of alarm clock he invented.

pa•tron•ize [pā′trən•īz′] *v.* **pa•tron•ized, pa•tron•iz•ing** To trade with regularly. My parents *patronize* small, local businesses instead of buying from the larger stores in the city.

pre•ci•sion [pri•sizh′ən] *n.* Exactness. *Precision* is important when one is working with tiny computer parts. *syn.* accuracy

a	add	o	odd	oi	oil
ā	ace	ō	open	ou	pout
â	care	ô	order	ng	ring
ä	palm	o͞o	took	th	thin
e	end	o͞o	pool	th	this
ē	equal	u	up	zh	vision
i	it	û	burn		
ī	ice	yo͞o	fuse		

ə = { a in *above*　　e in *sicken*　　i in *possible*
　　　o in *melon*　　u in *circus* }

prime [prīm] *adj.* First in value or excellence. The salesperson told us that the property was expensive because it was a *prime* piece of land. *syns.* best, choice, superior, top

pro·ject [prə·jekt′] *v.* **pro·ject·ed, pro·ject·ing** To cause a beam of light to cast an image onto a surface. If you shine a bright light through the photographic slide, you can *project* the picture onto a wall.

pro·long [prə·lông′] *v.* **pro·longed, pro·long·ing** To make longer in time or space. Thinking about what happened in the cafeteria today will only *prolong* your anger about the situation. *syns.* continue, lengthen

pro·sa·ic [prō·zā′ik] *adj.* Not interesting; ordinary. She decided that her life in a small town was *prosaic,* so she joined a dance company that toured the nation. *syns.* boring, dull

puck·er [puk′ər] *v.* **puck·ered, puck·er·ing** To gather or draw up in small folds or wrinkles. When I bite into a very sour apple, I begin to shiver and my lips *pucker.*

Q

quar·rel [kwôr′əl] *v.* **quar·reled, quar·rel·ing** To take part in a dispute or argument. They began to *quarrel* over even the smallest of differences of opinion. *syns.* argue, clash, disagree, fight

R

ra·di·us [rā′dē·əs] *n.* A line from the center of a circle to its outer border; used to measure a circular area. Albert decided to plant flowers in a three-foot *radius* all around the tree. ▲

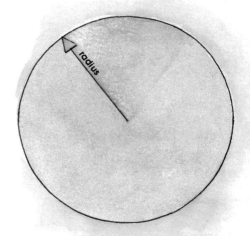

rage [rāj] *n.* Violent anger; fury; wrath. The man was in a *rage* when he learned that someone had stolen his wallet. *syn.* frenzy

re·dis·cov·er [rē′dis·kuv′ər] *v.* **re·dis·cov·ered, re·dis·cov·er·ing** To learn or find out again. I hope my mother will *rediscover* the joys of kite-flying when she takes us to the park on Saturday.

ren·o·vate [ren′ə·vāt′] *v.* **ren·o·vat·ed, ren·o·vat·ing** To make as good as new; repair. The city will *renovate* the historic house and turn it into a museum. *syns.* fix, renew

re·vi·tal·ize [rē·vīt′əl·īz′] *v.*
re·vi·tal·ized, re·vi·tal·iz·ing
To give new life to. The city has put aside money to *revitalize* the downtown areas that are becoming rundown.

ruse [rōoz] *n.* An action or trick intended to mislead or deceive. Janice's clever *ruse* to get out of doing her chores did not work because Mother knew that she wasn't really sick. *syn.* plot, scheme

S

sab·o·tage [sab′ə·tazh′] *v.*
sab·o·taged, sab·o·tag·ing To interfere with a country's war effort by deliberately destroying key items. The enemy tried to *sabotage* the air raid by substituting water for jet fuel.

skein [skān] *n.* A quantity of yarn or thread wound into a loose coil. Mother checked each *skein* of yarn to see that it was the same color as the others she would use for the sweater. ▲

sleuth [slōōth] *n.* A detective. My solution to the mystery in the movie changed each time the *sleuth* uncovered a new clue. *syn.* investigator

speech im·ped·i·ment [spēch im·ped′ə·mənt] *n.* A physical condition that makes normal speech difficult. My father has a *speech impediment* and has difficulty saying the letter "l" properly.

stim·u·la·tion [stim′yə·lā′shən] *n.* The condition of being roused to activity. Our reading teacher suggested library books we could read during the summer for mental *stimulation. syn.* excitement

sur·vey [sûr′vā′] *n.* A brief but thorough study. The cafeteria took a *survey* of the students about healthful foods they might like for lunch. *syns.* poll, vote ▲

a	add	o	odd	oi	oil
ā	ace	ō	open	ou	pout
â	care	ô	order	ng	ring
ä	palm	o͞o	took	th	thin
e	end	o͞o	pool	t͟h	this
ē	equal	u	up	zh	vision
i	it	û	burn		
ī	ice	yo͞o	fuse		

ə = { a in *above*   e in *sicken*   i in *possible*
      { o in *melon*   u in *circus*

sus•pi•cion [sə•spish′ən] *n.* A feeling that something is wrong. We all had a *suspicion* that something was wrong at our house when we saw the fire truck rushing up our street.

T

thread [thred] *n.* The spiral or curving groove cut into a screw or nut. When the *thread* inside the lid bent, the lid no longer screwed onto the jar tightly. ▲

tink•er [tingk′ər] *v.* **tink•ered, tink•er•ing** To work on or repair. Juan likes to *tinker* with old radios to try to fix them.

tongue [tung] *n.* A language or dialect. Raul speaks English well, but his native *tongue* is Spanish. *syn.* speech

trans•at•lan•tic [trans′ət•lan′tik] *adj.* Across or crossing the Atlantic Ocean. In the 1800s, it took most ships at least three weeks to make a *transatlantic* voyage.

trans•mit•ter [trans•mit′ər] *n.* A device that sends out a message by means of electricity or electromagnetic waves. She used the radio *transmitter* to send a message all the way to Australia.

U

un•mer•ci•ful•ly [un•mûr′sə•fə•lē] *adv.* In a way that shows cruelty. My friends teased me *unmercifully* about missing that easy free throw.

un•pre•dict•a•ble [un′pri•dik′tə•bəl] *adj.* Not able to be known in advance. Because the path of a tornado is *unpredictable*, everyone nearby should take shelter.

V

vet•er•an [vet′ər•ən] *n.* A former member of the armed forces. My grandfather is a *veteran* of World War II.

vet•er•i•nar•i•an [vet′ər•ə•nâr′ē•ən] *n.* A doctor who treats animals. When my kitten was sick, I took him to a *veterinarian* for treatment.

wand [wond] *n.* A thin stick or rod. The magician waved her *wand*, and the rabbit seemed to disappear. ▲

Art Acknowledgments

Fian Arroyo: 40–51; Jim Campbell: 54–65; Vince Caputo: 172–179; Thomas Gonzalez: 66–77; R. Mark Heath: 80–95; Cary Henrie: 200–211; Mitchell Hooks: 4–13; Chet Jezierski: 138–155; Bob Jones: 130–137; Bill Mayer: 38–39, 198–199; John Nelson: 110–115; Carol Norby: 156–157; Randy South: 17–25; Cliff Spohn: 28–37; Cathy Trachok: 158–168; Tina Zeno: 172 (title).

Photographs

Cover, Masa Vemura/TSW/Click, Chicago; iv, Famous People Players; vii, Scott Dietrich/TSW/Click, Chicago; viii, Alice Terry; x, The Bettman Archive; xi, HBJ Photo/Gabor Demjun & Roy Kirby/Aperture, Inc.; 2, Famous People Players; 4, Famous People Players, 5, Famous People Players; 6, Raeanne Rubenstein/Telephoto; 9, Raeanne Rubenstein/Telephoto; 10, Raeanne Rubestein/Telephoto; 12(all), Famous People Players; 13(top to bottom), Famous People Players, Raeanne Rubenstein/Telephoto, Famous People Players,, Famous People Players, Famous People Players, Raeanne Rubenstein/Telephoto, Raeanne Rubenstein/Telephoto, Raeanne Rubenstein/Telephoto, Raeanne Rubenstein/Telephoto; Raeanne Rubenstein/Telephoto; 14, Raeanne Rubenstein/Telephoto; 36, Mrs. Winifred Latimer Norman; 36–37, HBJ Photo/Jim Davie; 53 (t), Melinda Berge/Bruce Coleman, Inc.; 53 (b), Science Photo Library/Photo Researchers; 78–79, Science Photo Library/Photo Researchers, HBJ Photo/© 1961 California Institute of Technology and Carnegie Institution of Washington/Hale Observatories; 96(l), Scott Dietrich/TSW/Click, Chicago; 96(r), Jim Pickerell/FPG; 96–97, Robert Ashe/Stock Imagery; 97 (l), Melinda Berge/Bruce Coleman, Inc.; 97(r), Doris DeWitt/TSW/Click, Chicago; 98–99, Scott Dietrich/TSW/Click, Chicago; 98, Eric Roth/The Picture Cube; 99, Eunice Harris/The Picture Cube; 100–101, Jim Pickerell/FPG; 100, Frank Cezus/TSW/Click, Chicago; 101, Peter Pearson/TSW/Click, Chicago; 102–103, Robert Ashe/Stock Imagery; 102, Robert King/TSW/After-Image; 103, Barry Staver; 104–105, Melinda Berge/Bruce Coleman, Inc.; 104, David Noble/FPG; 105, Mitchell L. Osborne; 106–107, Doris DeWitt/TSW/Click, Chicago; 106, James Blank/Bruce Coleman, Inc.; 107, George Rockwin/Bruce Coleman, Inc.; 108 (l), Scott Dietrick/TSW/Click, Chicago; 108 (c), Jim Pickerell/FPG; 108(r), Robert Ashe/Stock Imagery; 118–129 (All spreads), HBJ Photo/Earl Kogler; 118–119(all), Julinna Oxley; 120, Julinna Oxley; 122, Alice Terry; 126, Alice Terry; 127(l), Alice Terry; 127(r), Rob Nelson; 128, courtesy, Alice Terry; 170, Yeoman Films Archives/Shooting Star; 171, HBJ Photo/Gabor Demjen & Roy Kirby/Aperture, Inc.; 172–179, HBJ Photo/ © 1959 California Institute of Technology; 180–181, Yeoman Film Archives/Shooting Star; 180, HBJ Photo; 182–183, The Bettmann Archive; 183(top to bottom), Photofest, Photofest, Photofest, Frederick Lewis, Inc.; 184–185, Photofest; 185(all), Photofest; 186–187, Kobal Collection; 186(all), Photofest; 187(top to bottom), Photofest, Photofest, Frederick Lewis, Inc., Kobal Collection; 188–189, Photofest; 189(top to bottom) Photofest, Frederick Lewis, Inc., Photofest, Photofest, 190—191(Background), Photofest; 190–191(left to right), © 1977 Lucasfilm, Ltd., © 1980 Lucasfilm, Ltd., © 1980 Lucasfilm, Ltd., © 1980 Lucasfilm, Ltd., Frederick Lewis, Inc.; 192–193, Tri-Star Pictures, Inc.; 194–195(all), PIXAR/Lucasfilm/Paramount Pictures; 196, PIXAR/Lucasfilm/Paramount Pictures. 200–210, HBJ Photo Erik Arnesen; 212–213(Background), Craig Aurness/West Light; 212–213(Portraits), HBJ Photo/Gabor Demjen & Roy Kirby/Aperture, Inc.; 214–215(Background), HBJ Photo/Terry Sinclair; 214(Portrait), HBJ Photo/Gabor Demjen & Roy Kirby/Aperture, Inc.; 216–217(Background), Brian Milne/Animals Animals; 217(Portrait), HBJ Photo/Gabor Demjen & Roy Kirby/Aperture, Inc.; 218–219(Background), Stock Imagery; 219(Portrait), HBJ Photo/Gabor Demjen & Roy Kirby/Aperture, Inc.; 220–221(Background), Tony Stone Worldwide; 220(Portrait), HBJ Photo/Gabor Demjen & Roy Kirby/Aperture, Inc.